Special Thanks

To Echo Foronda at Insomniart Studios for the creation of this book

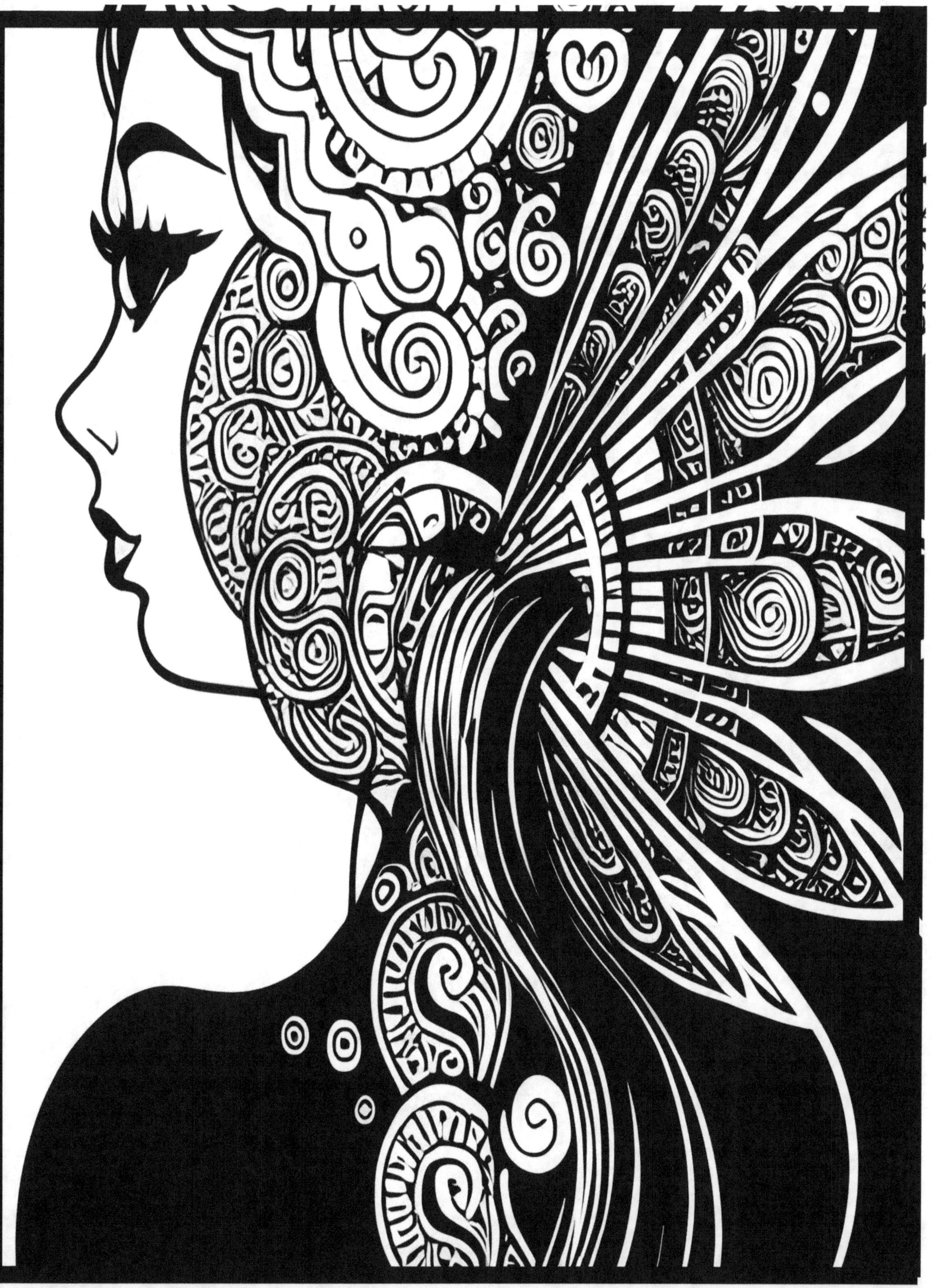

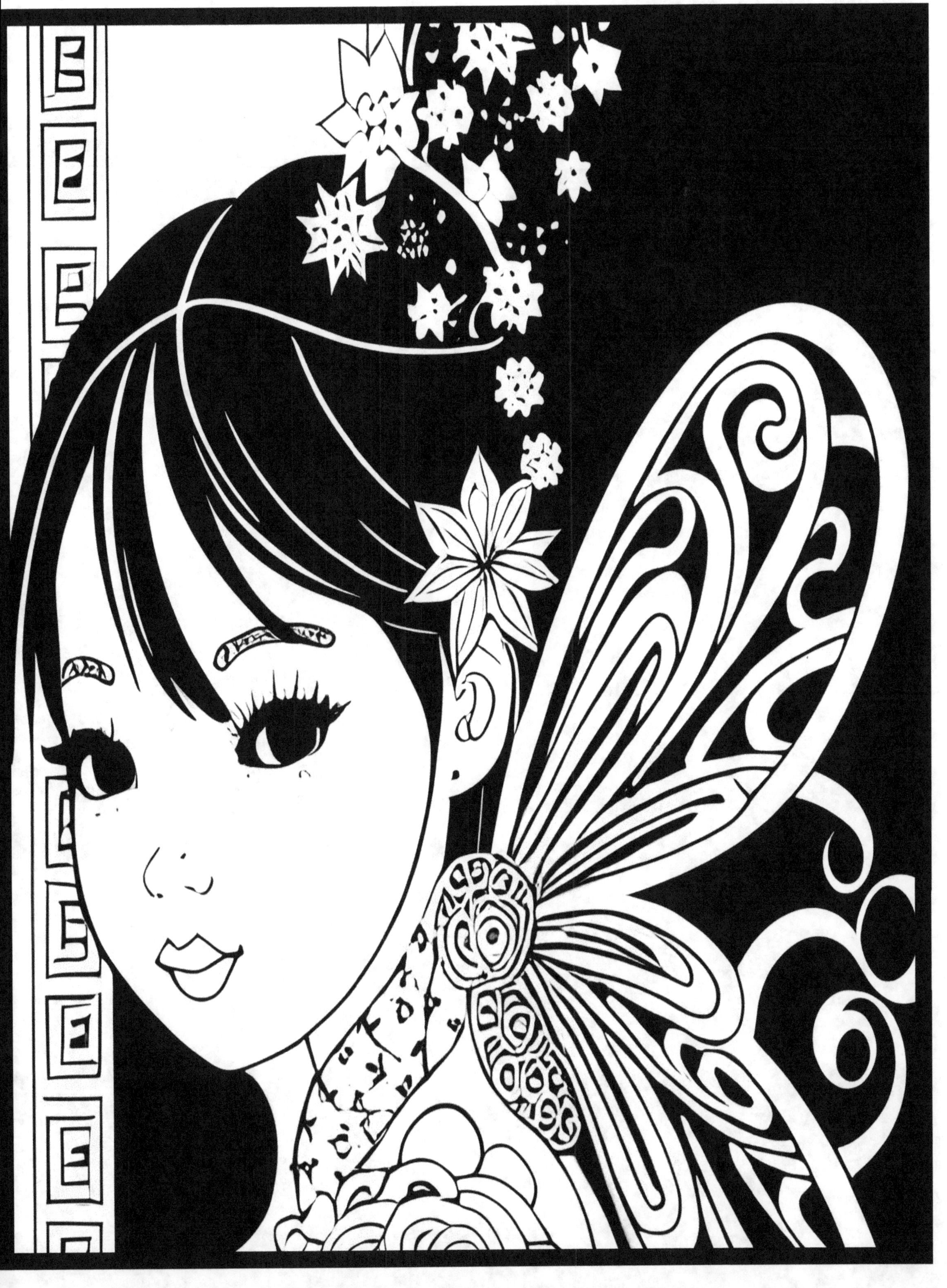

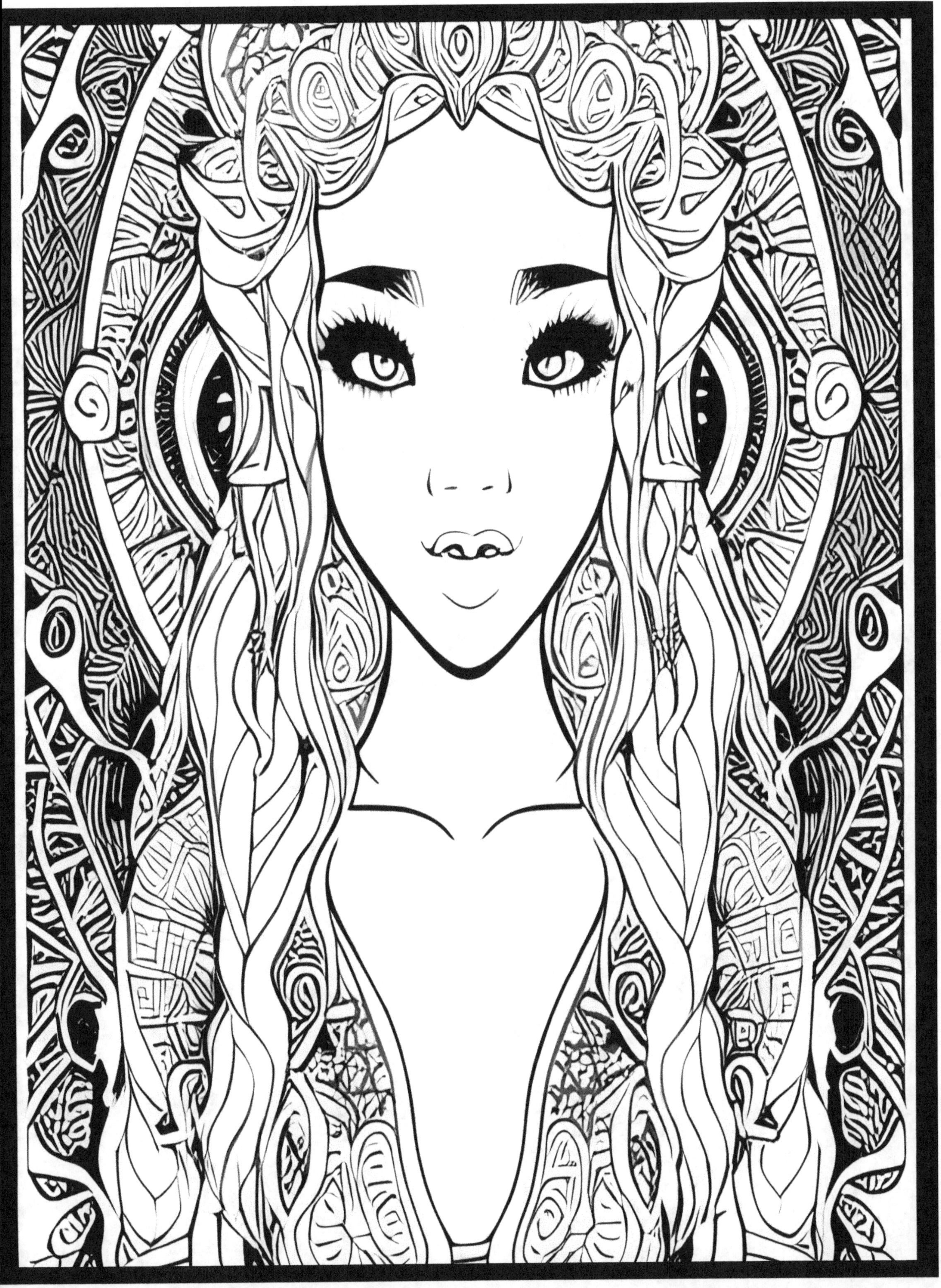

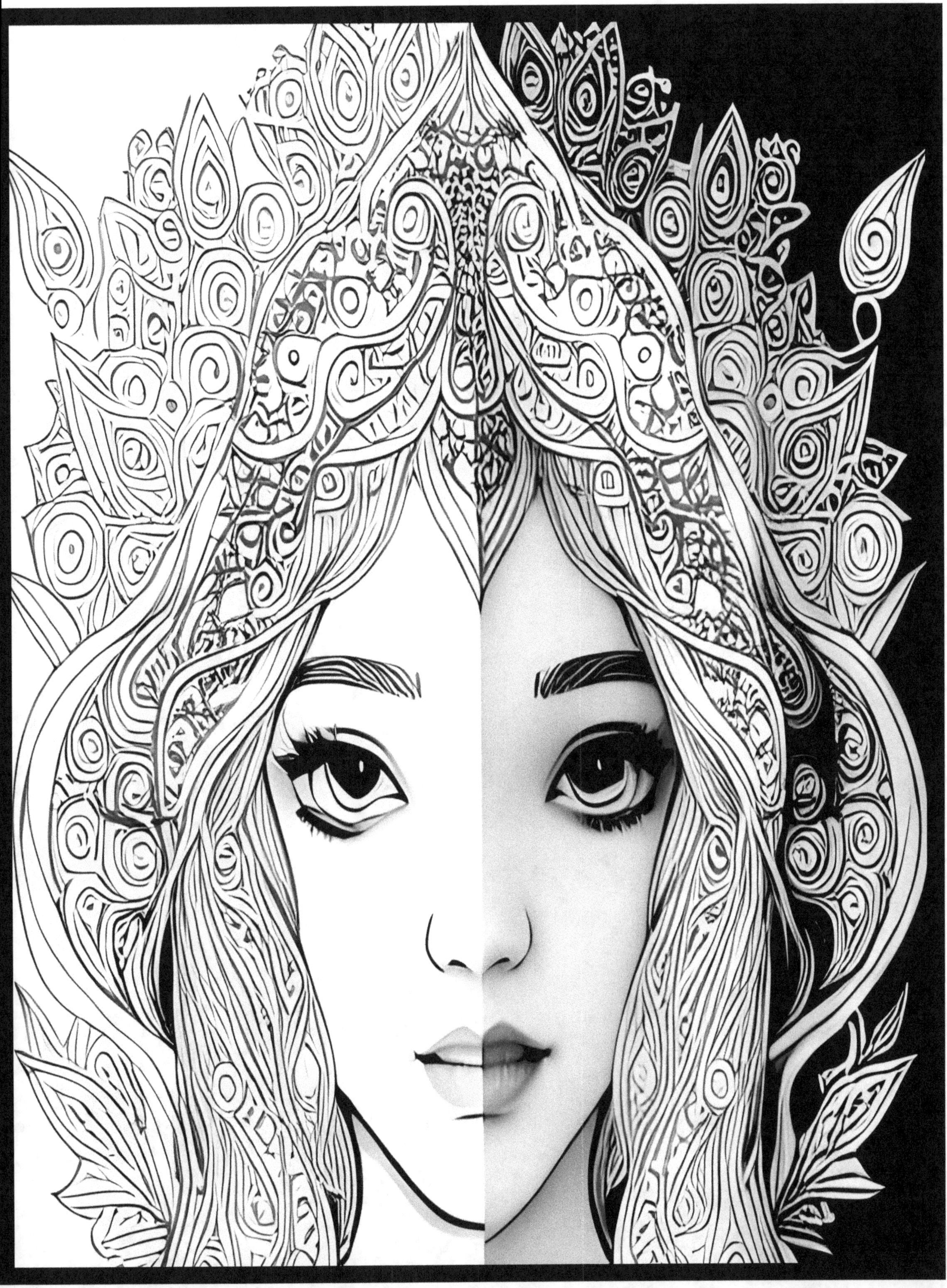

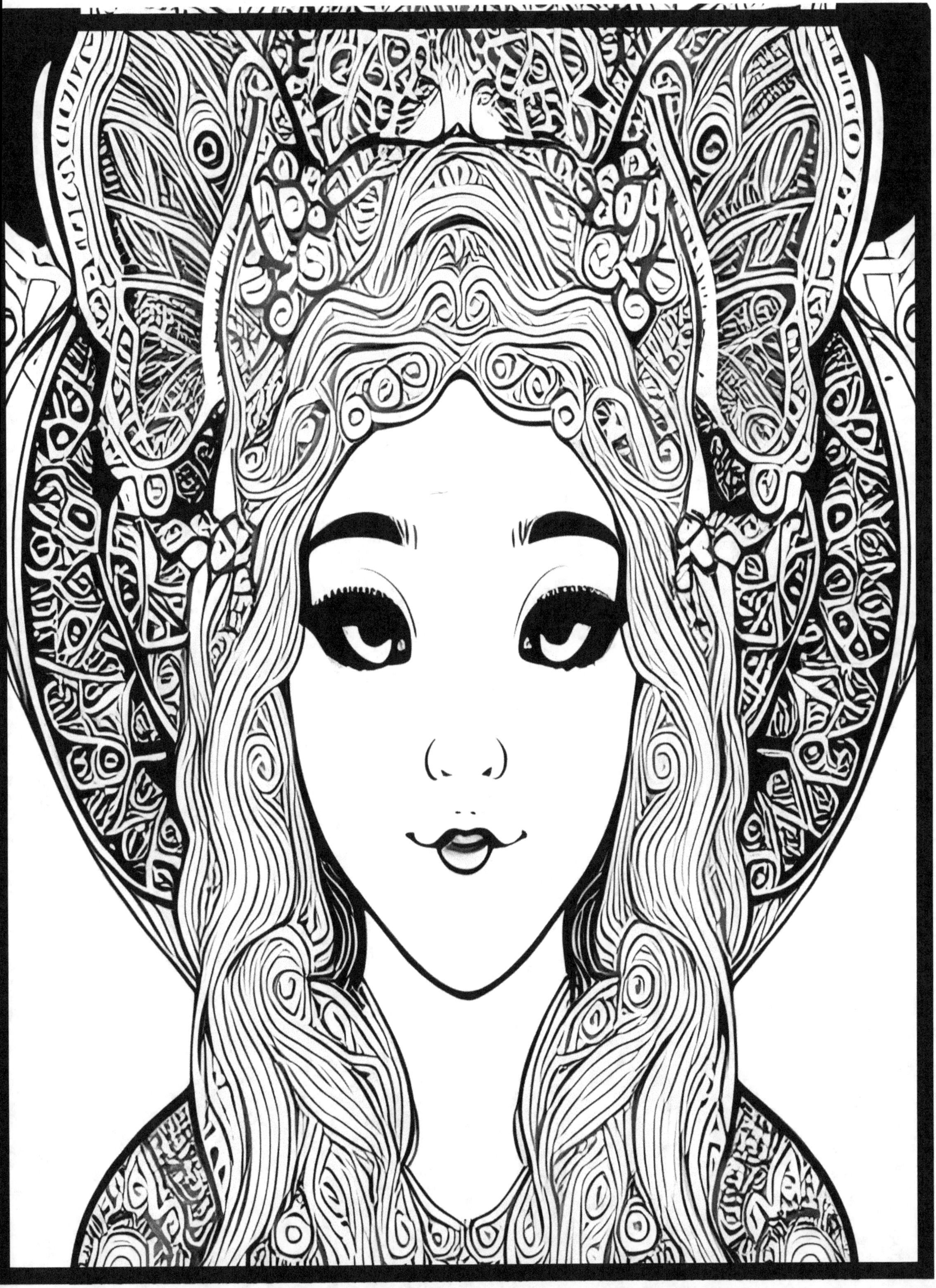

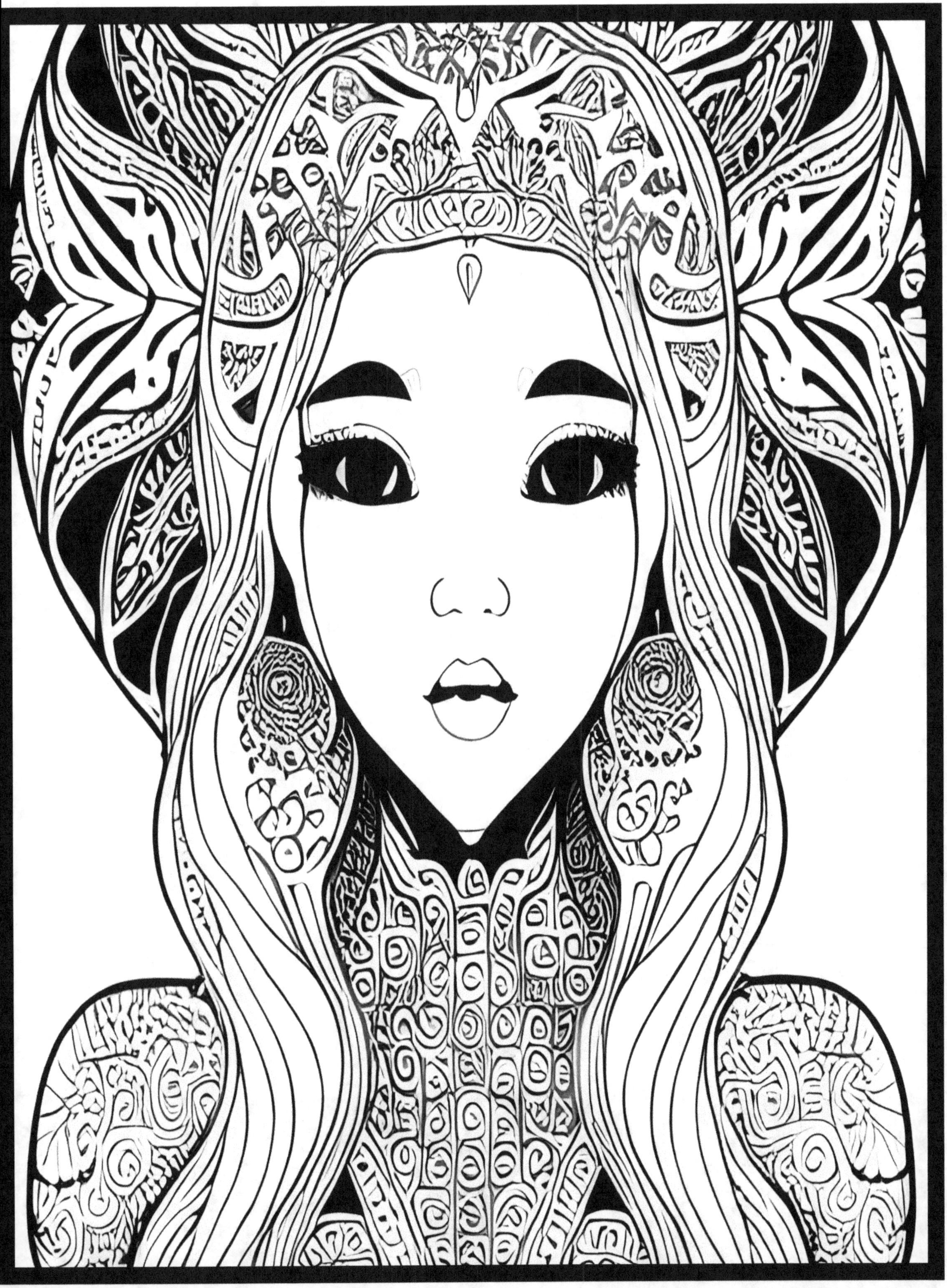

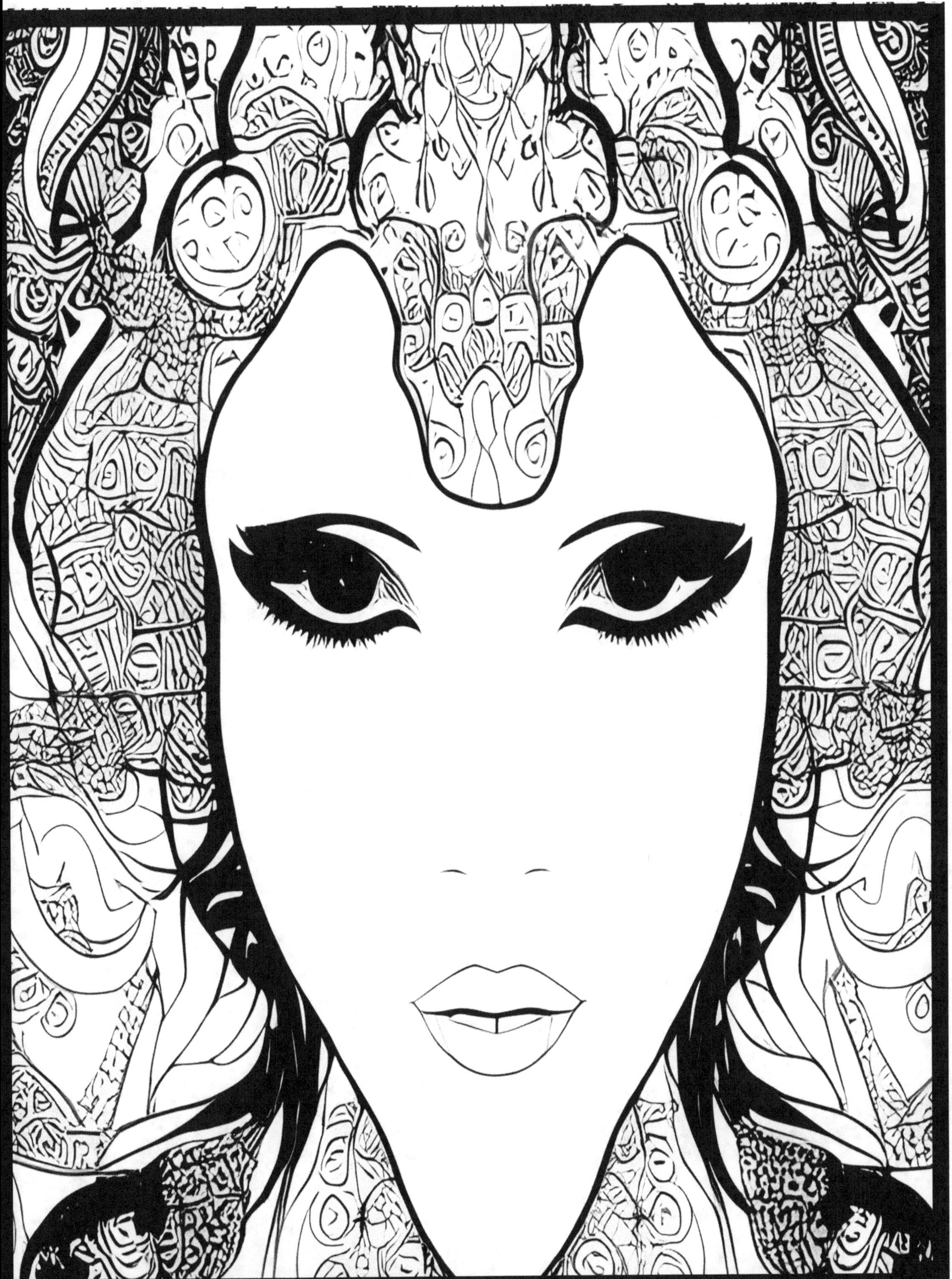

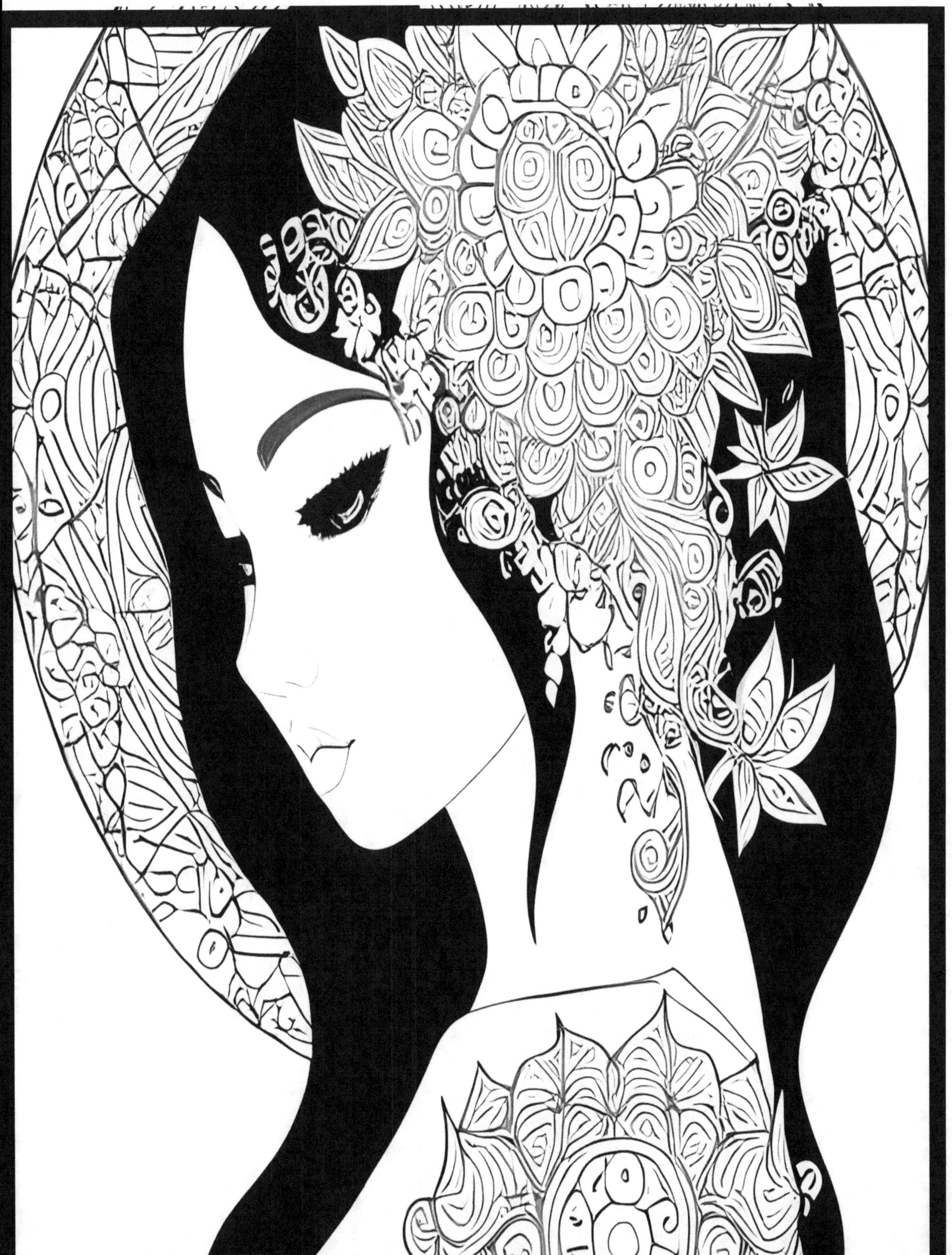

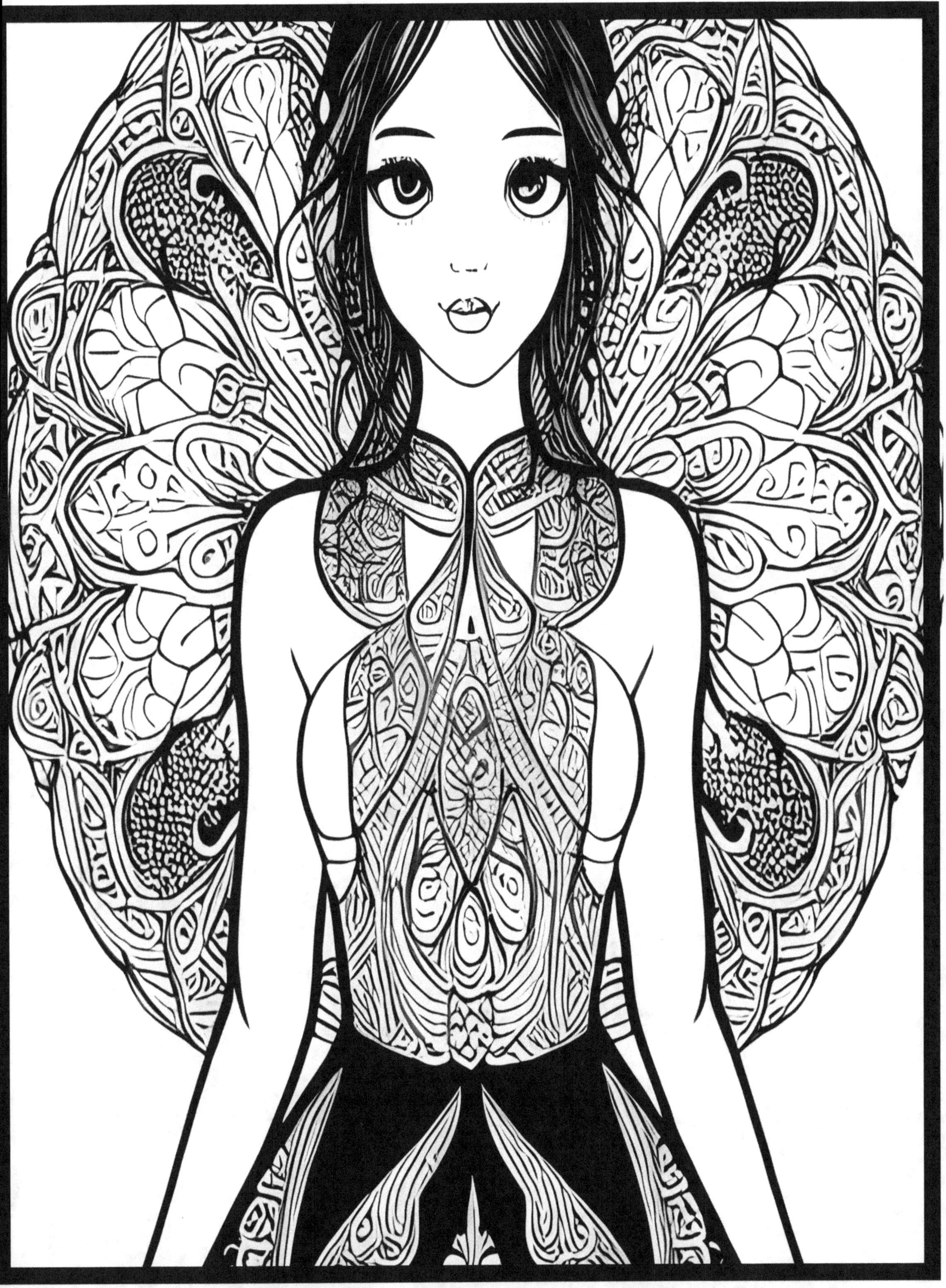

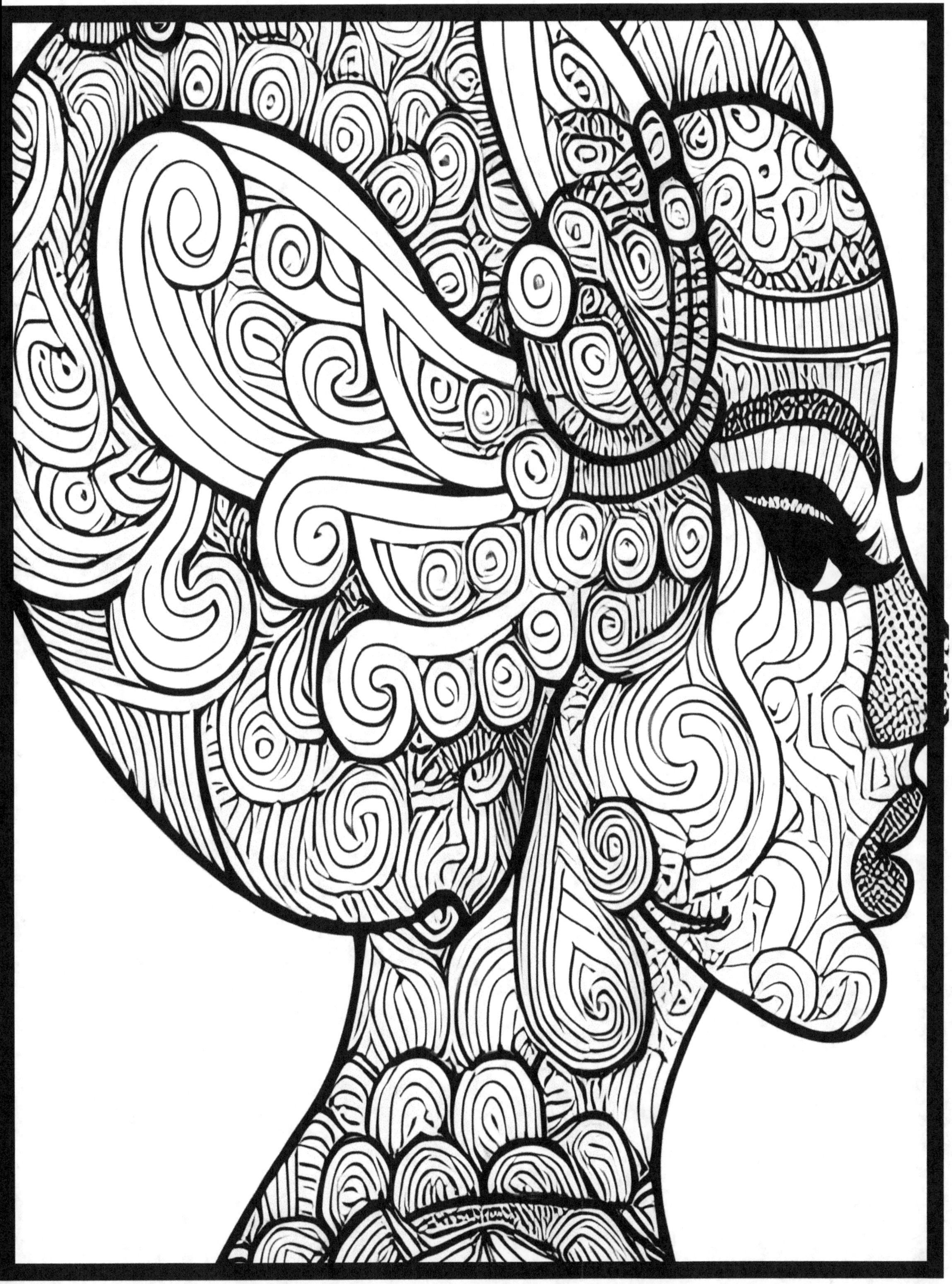

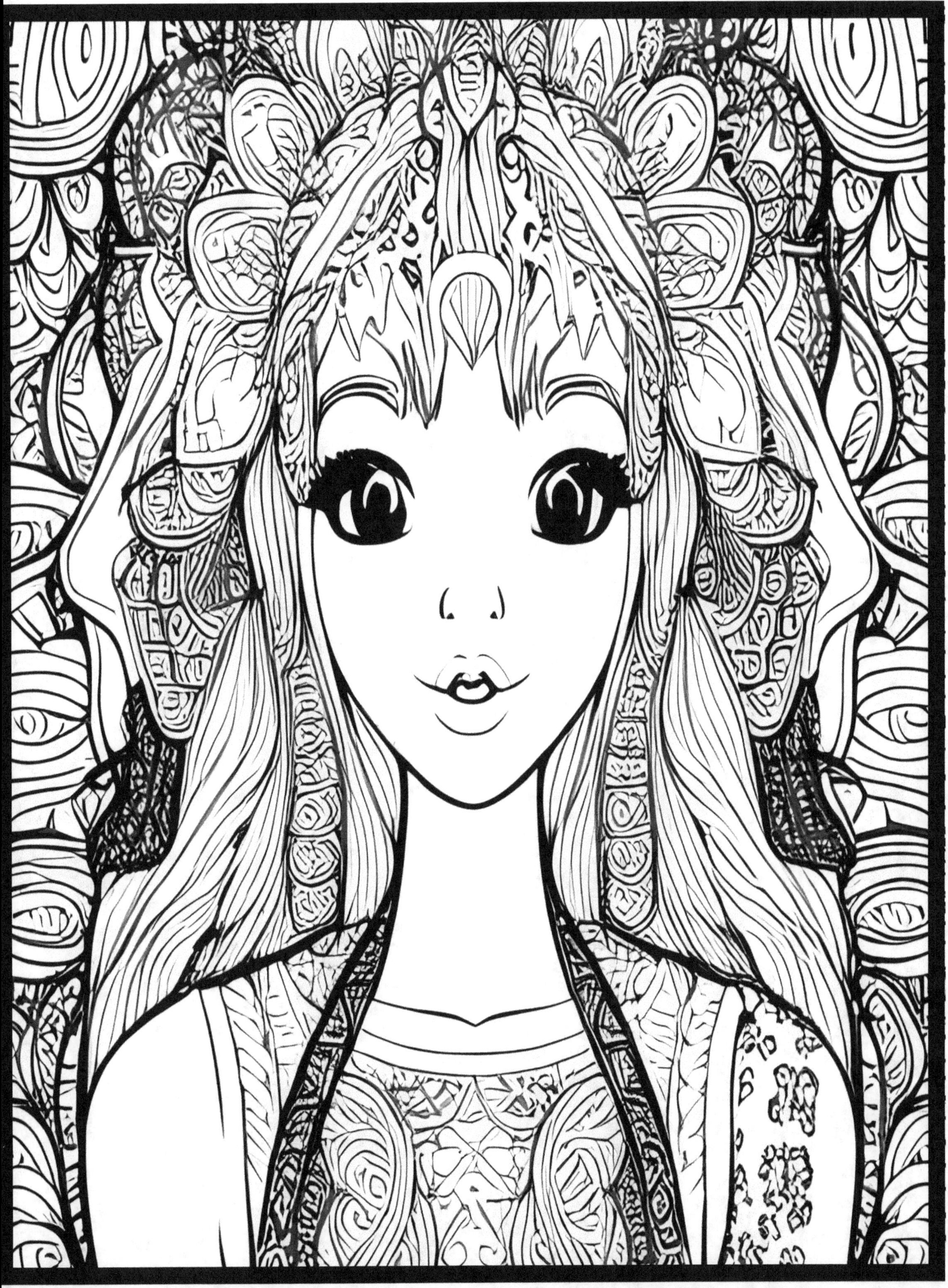

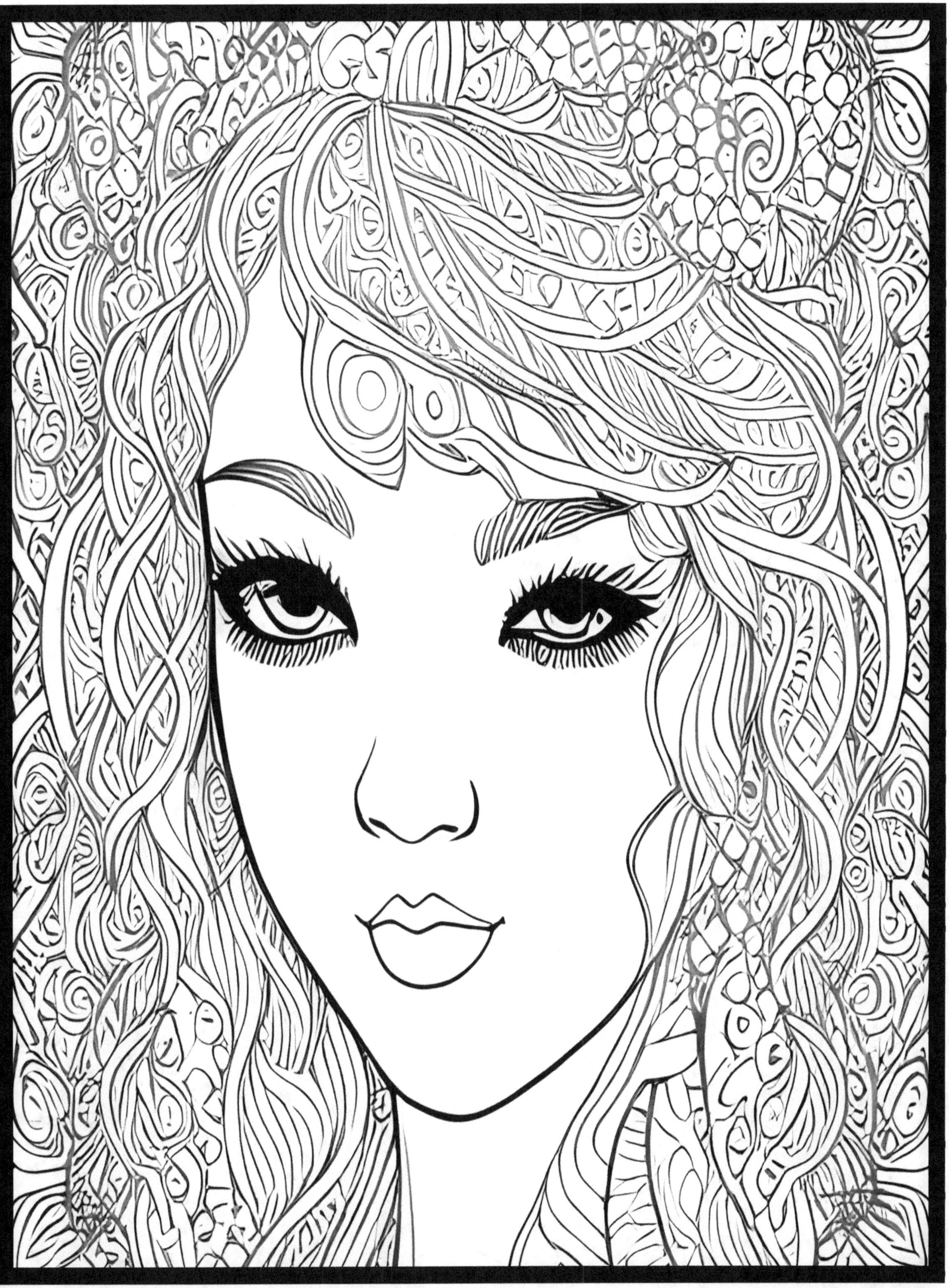

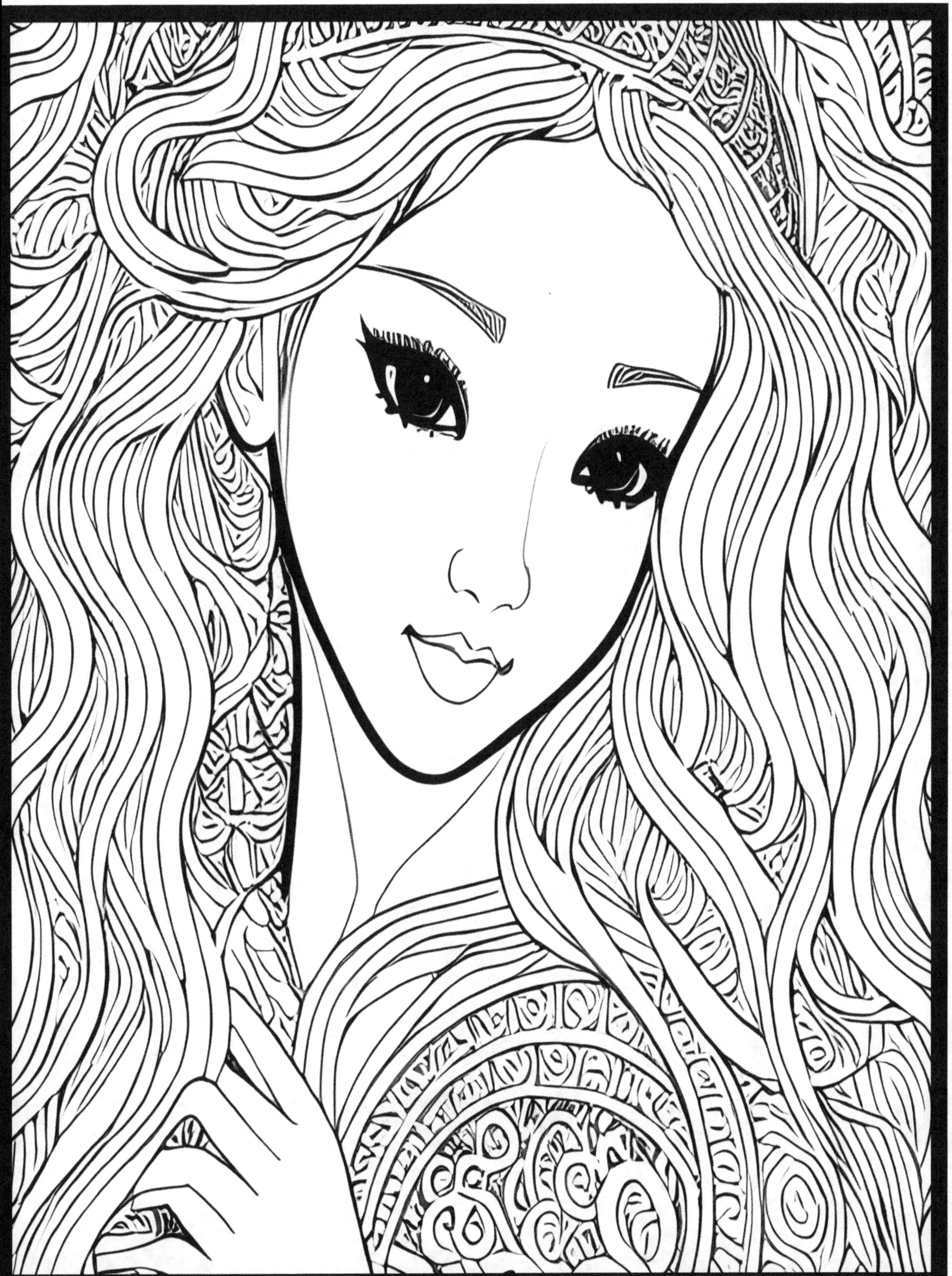

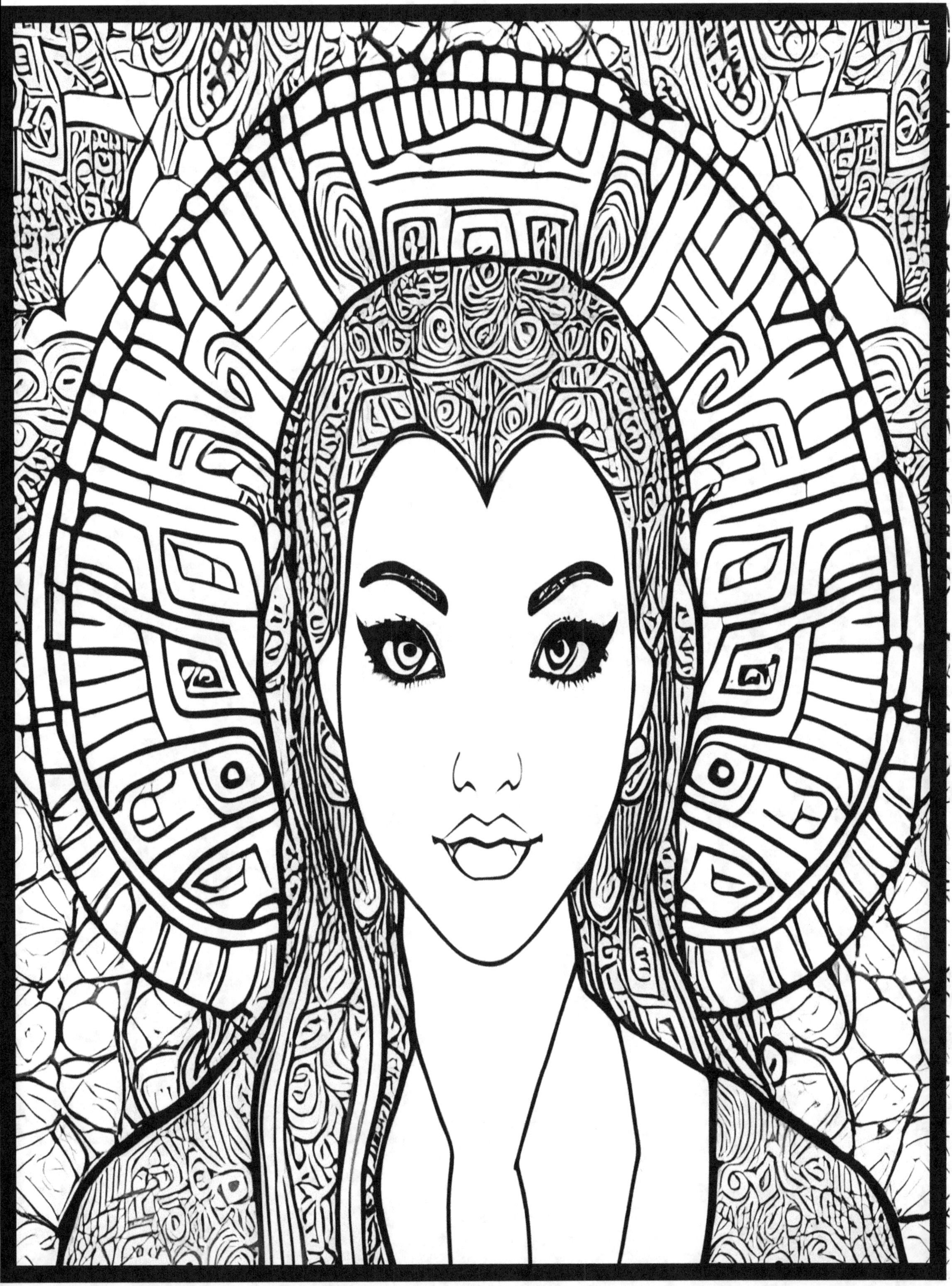

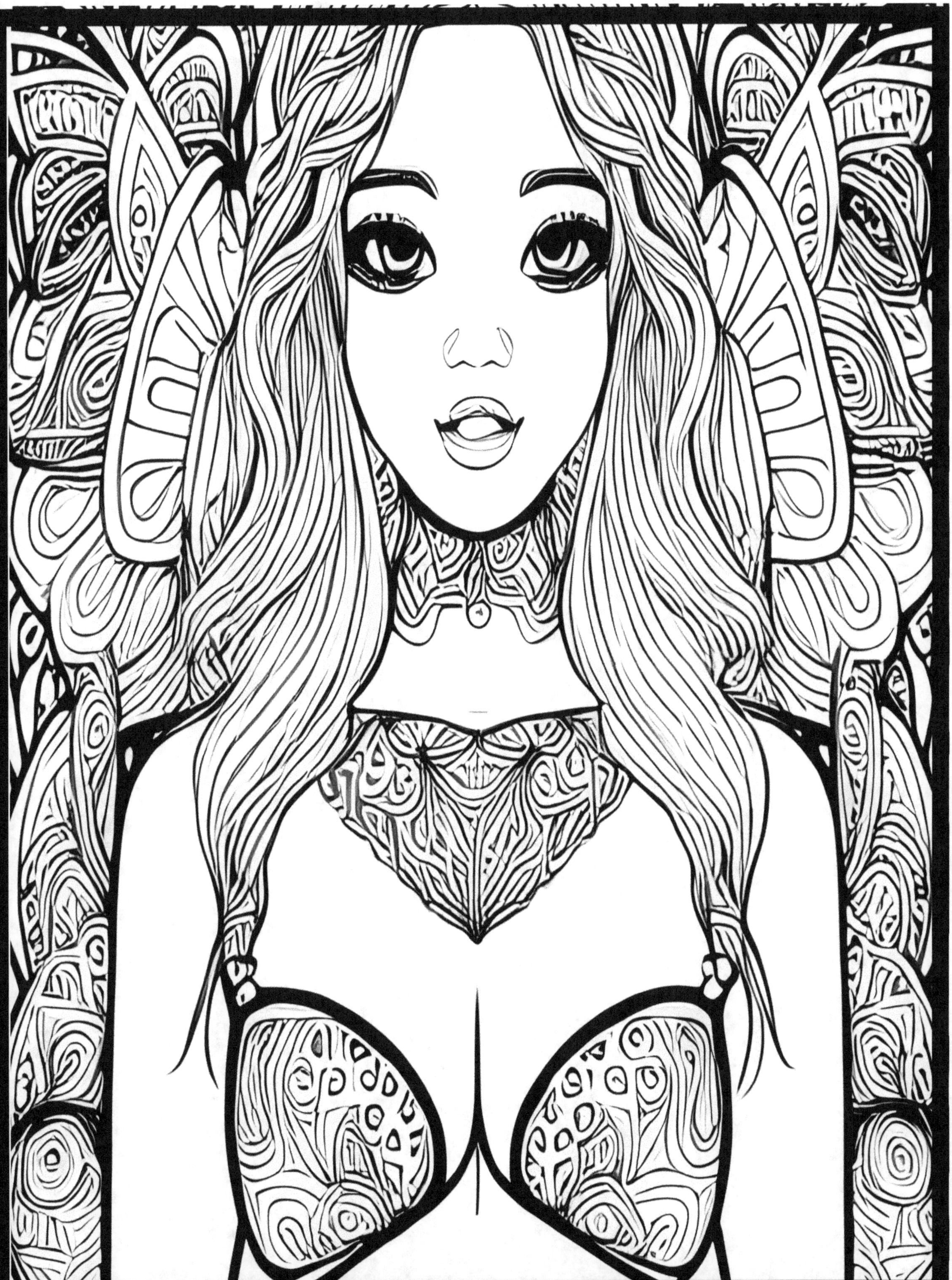

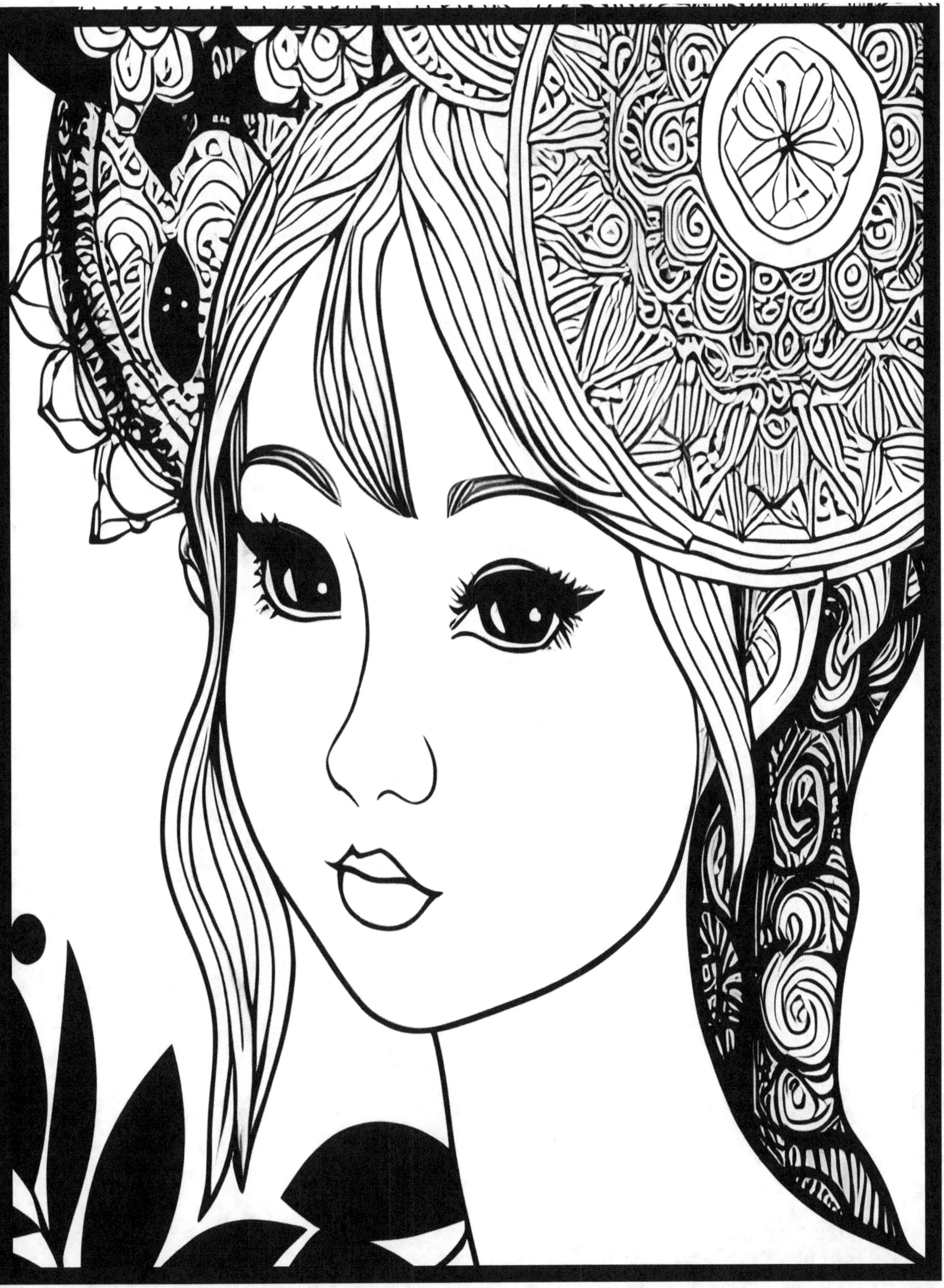

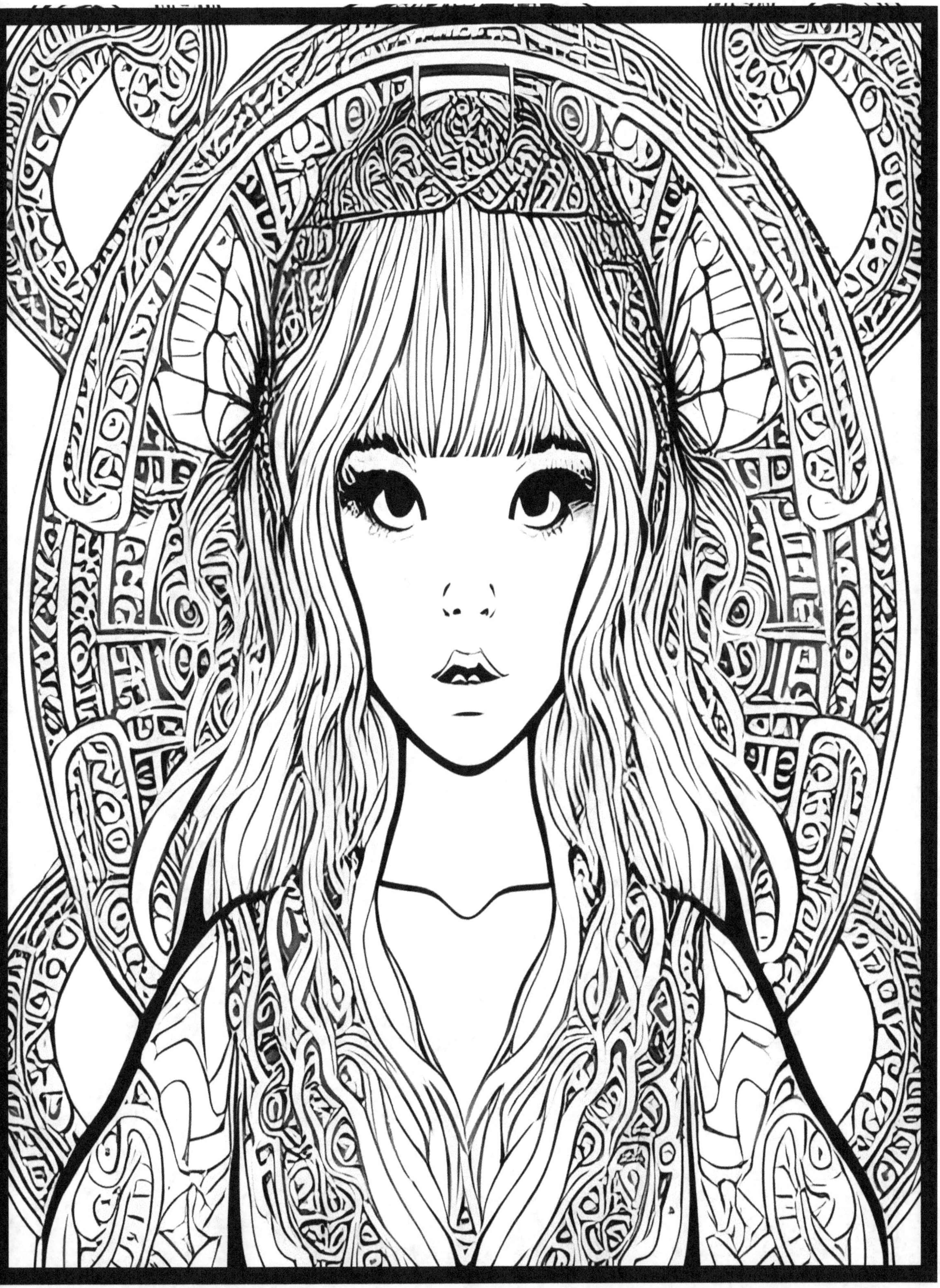

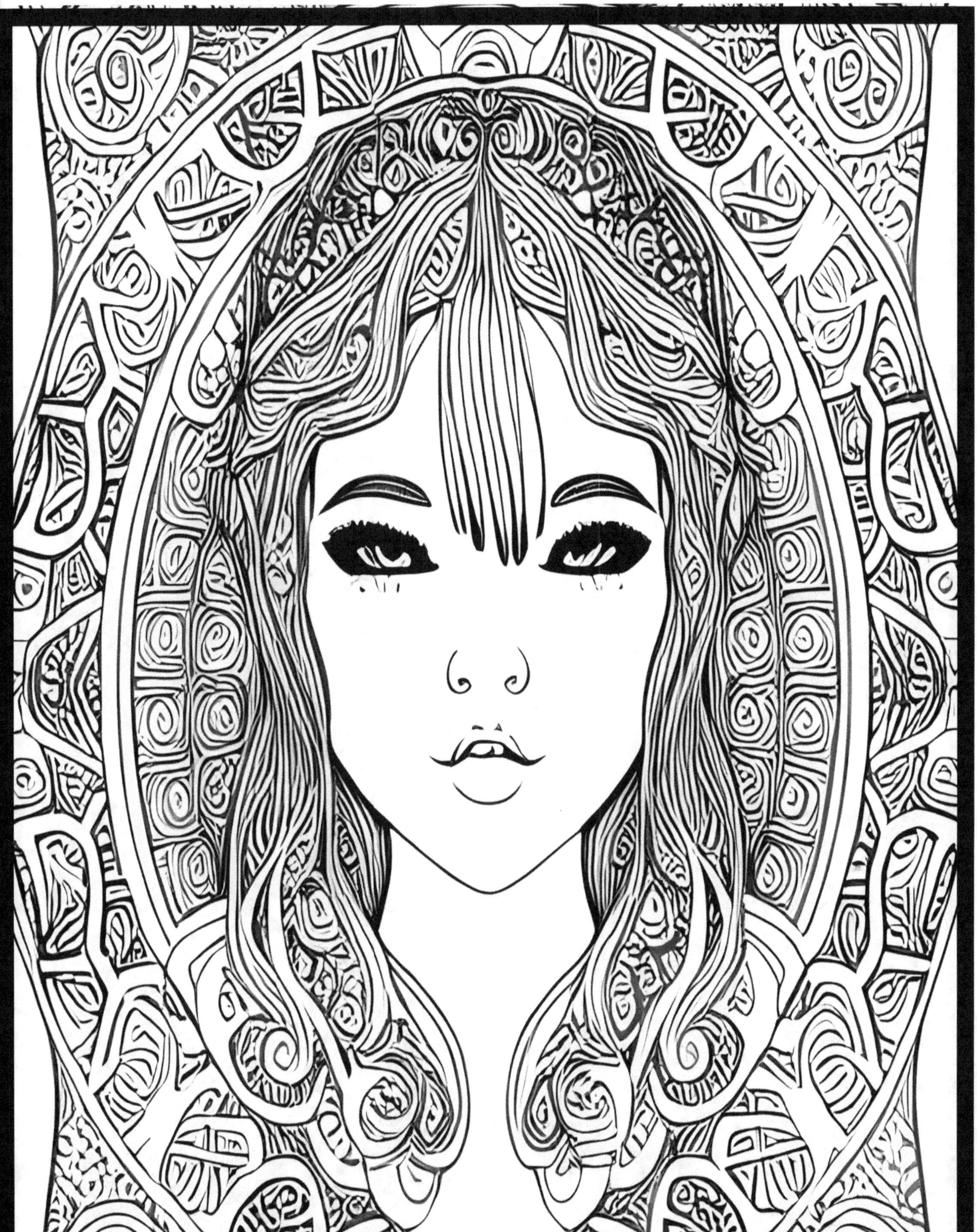

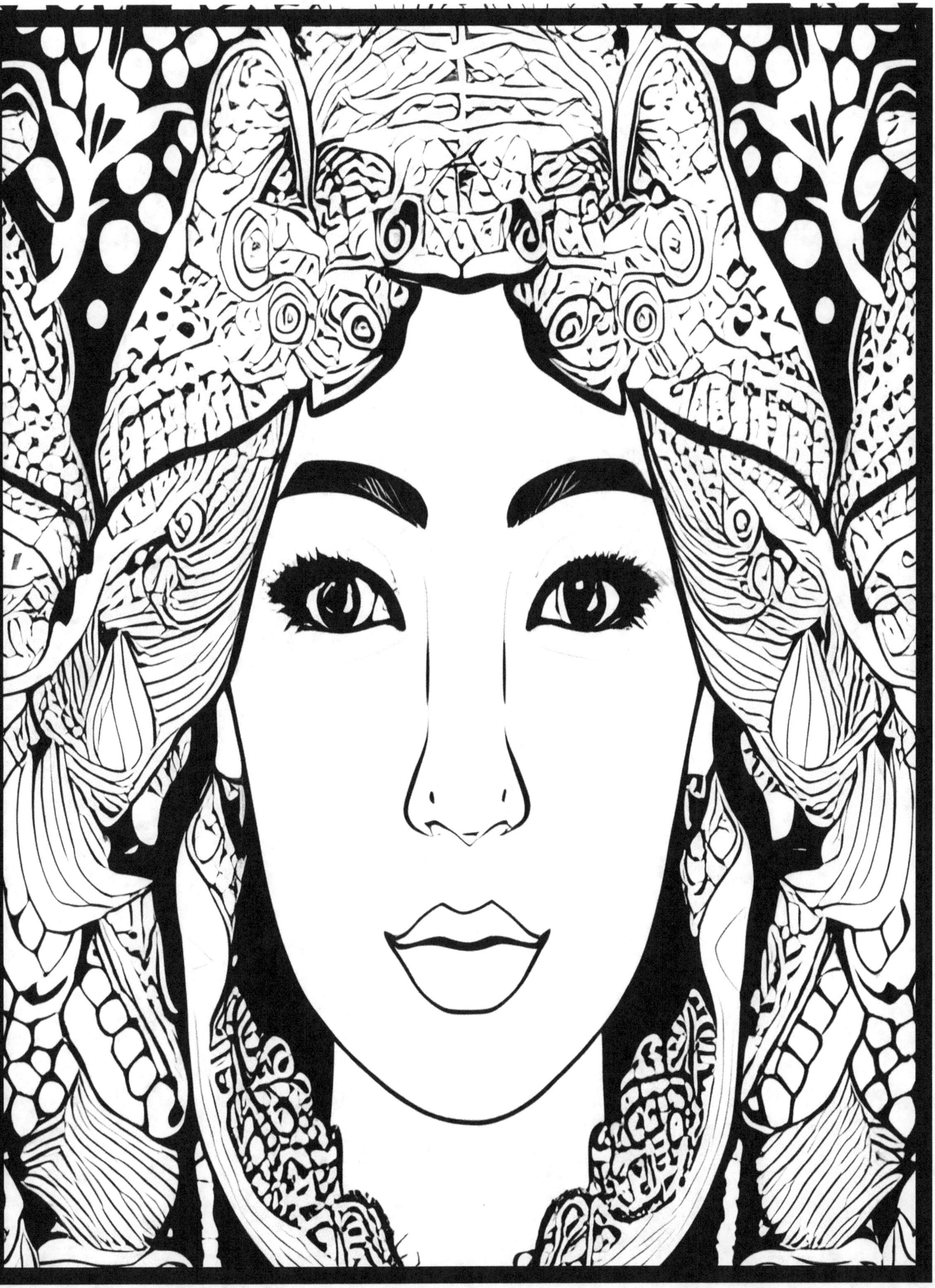

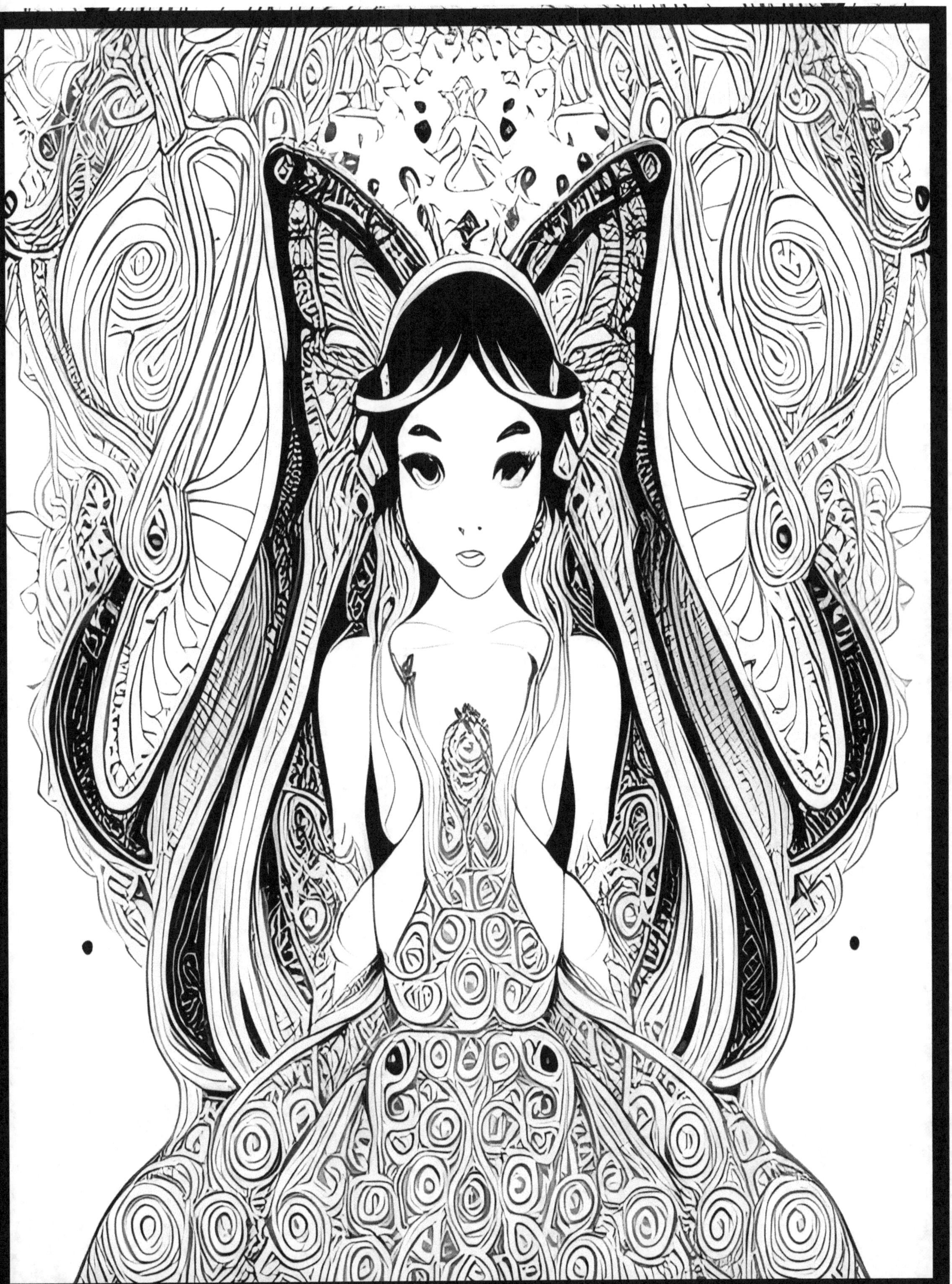

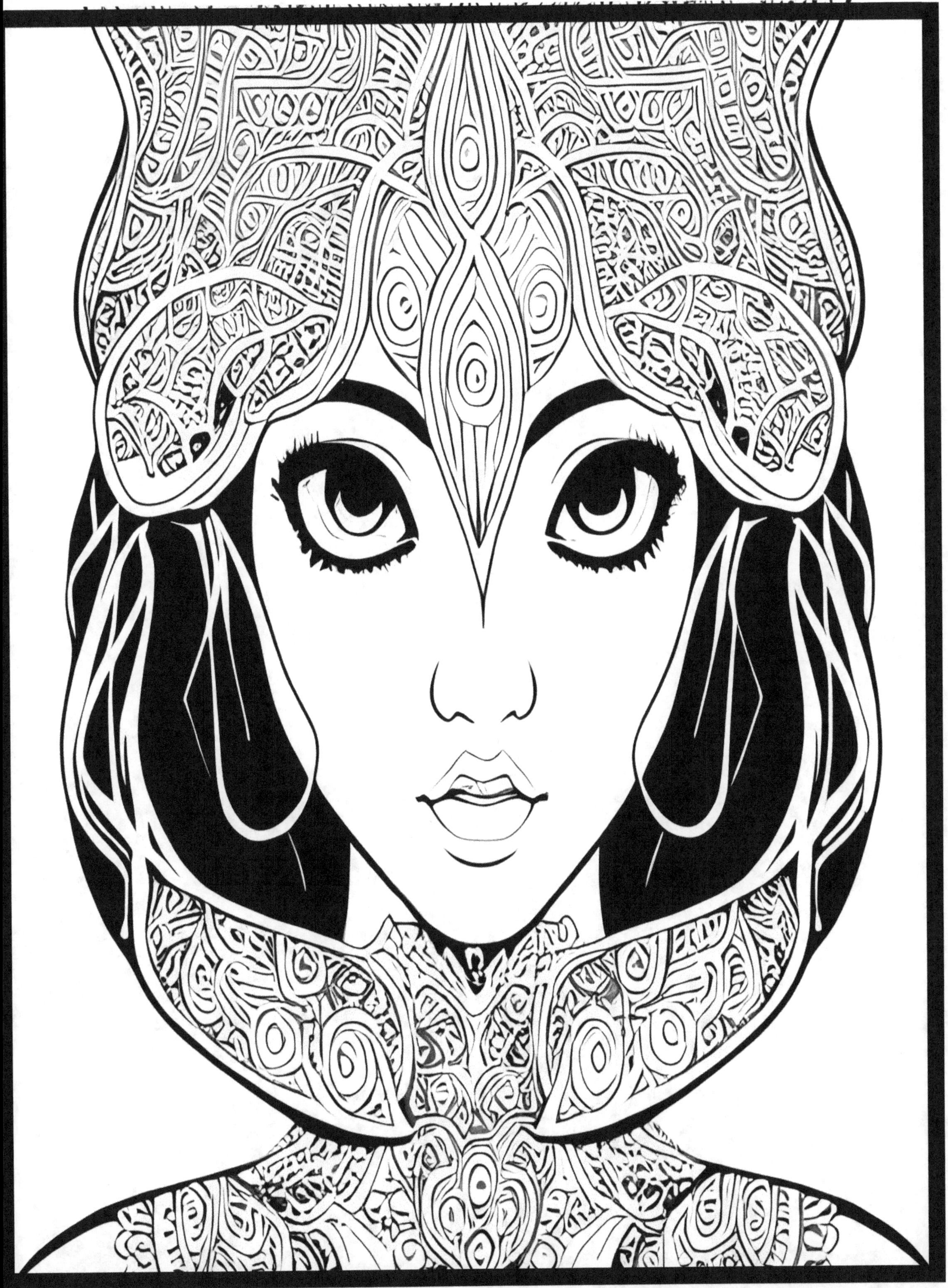

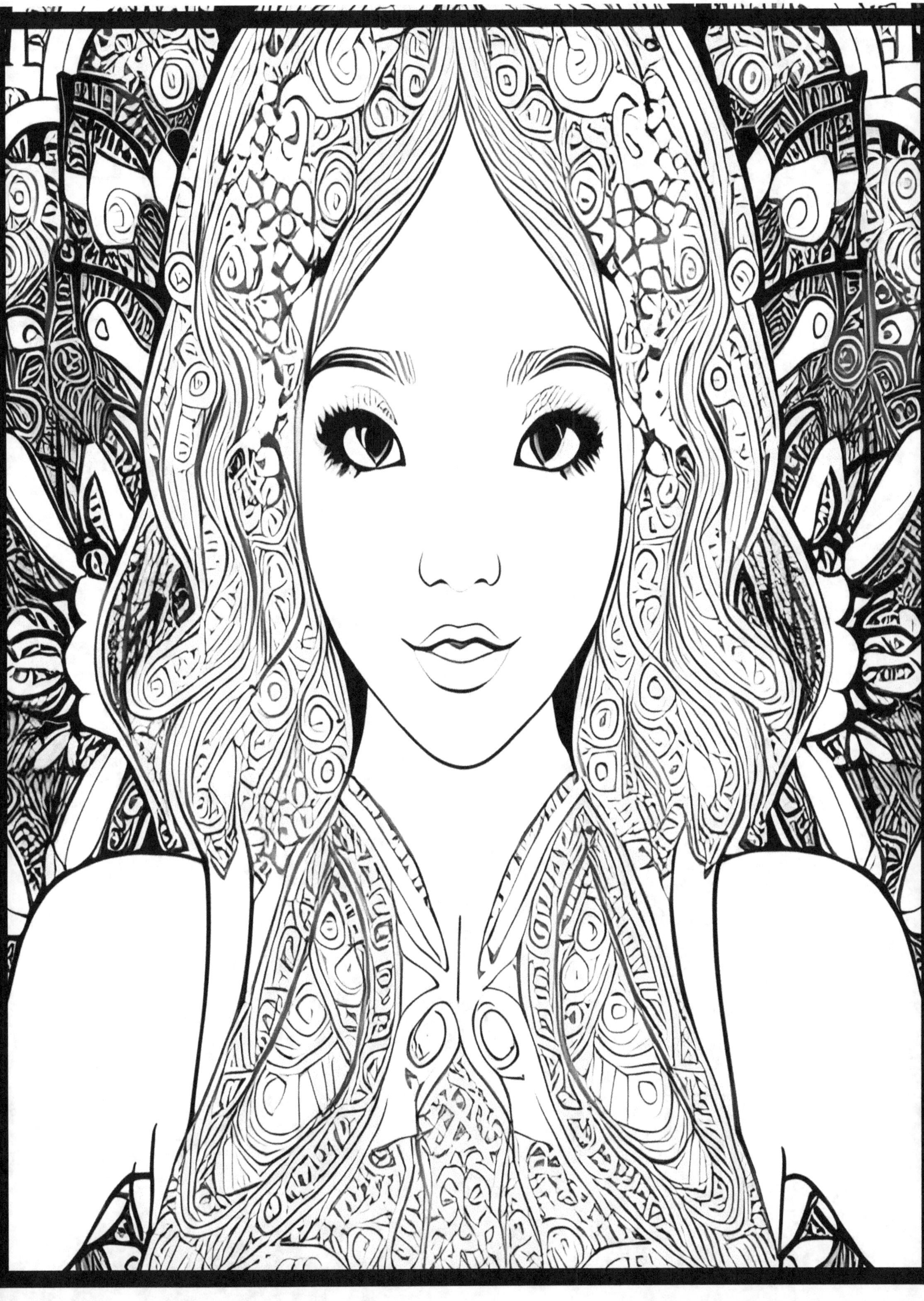

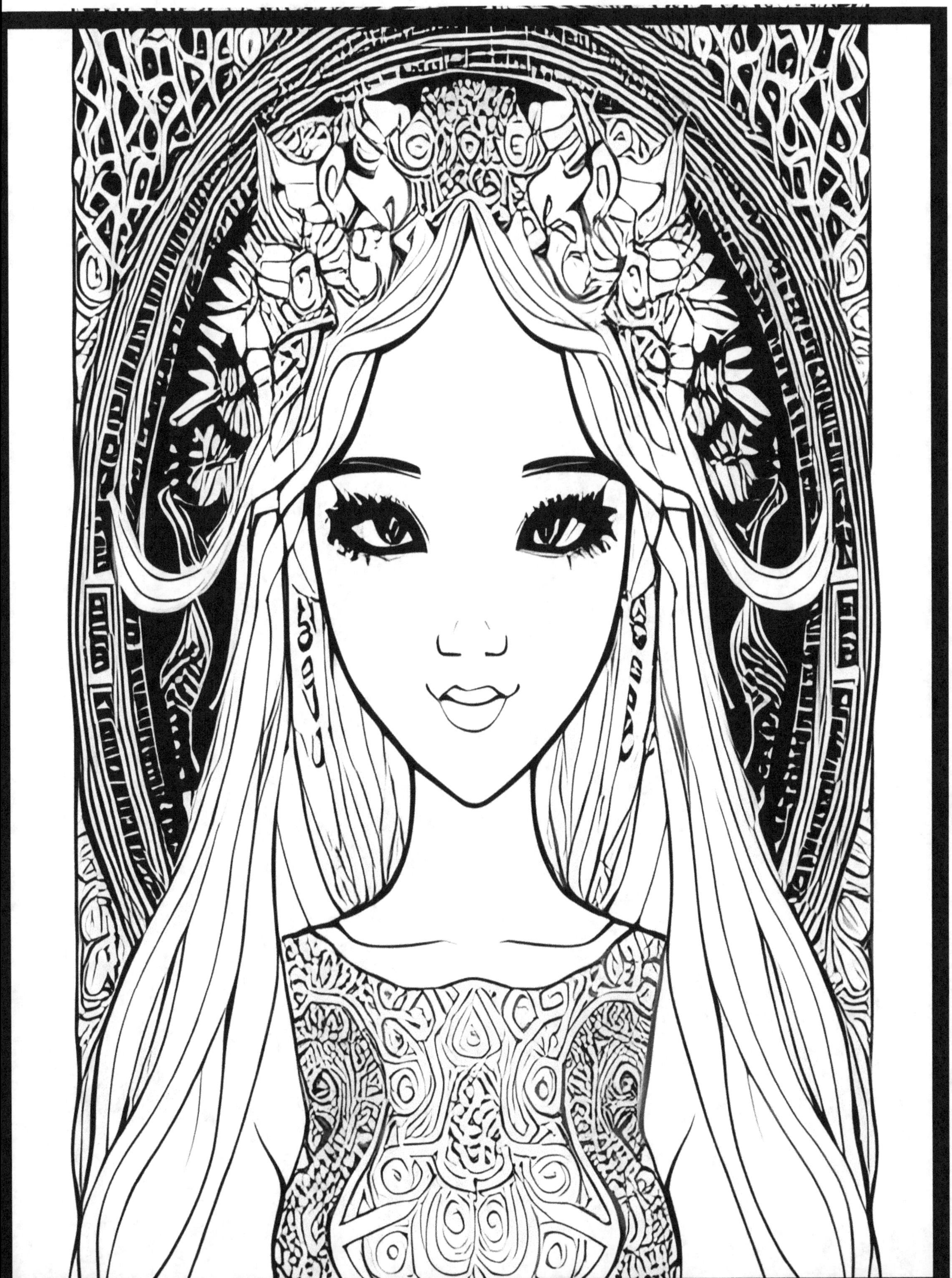

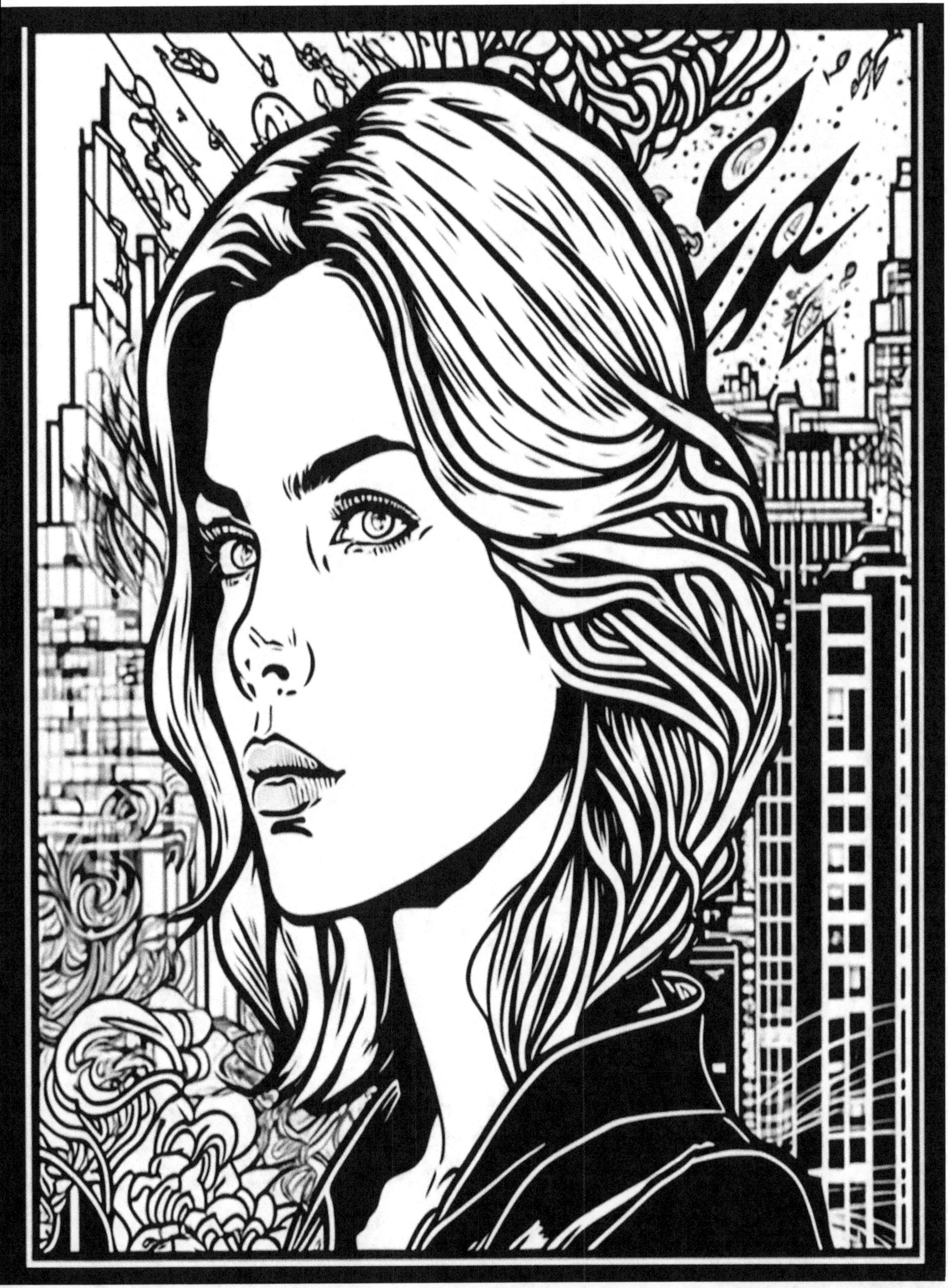

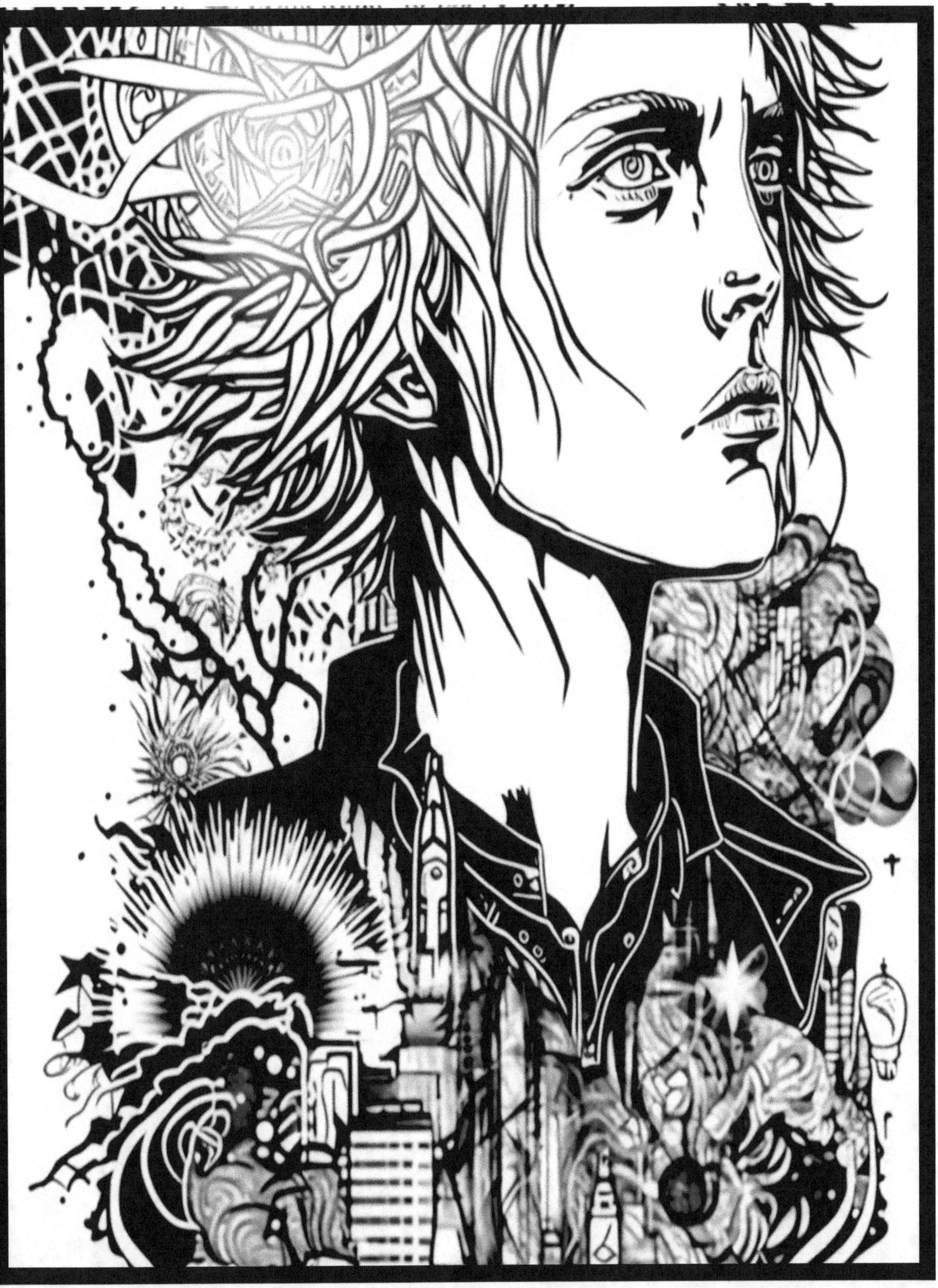

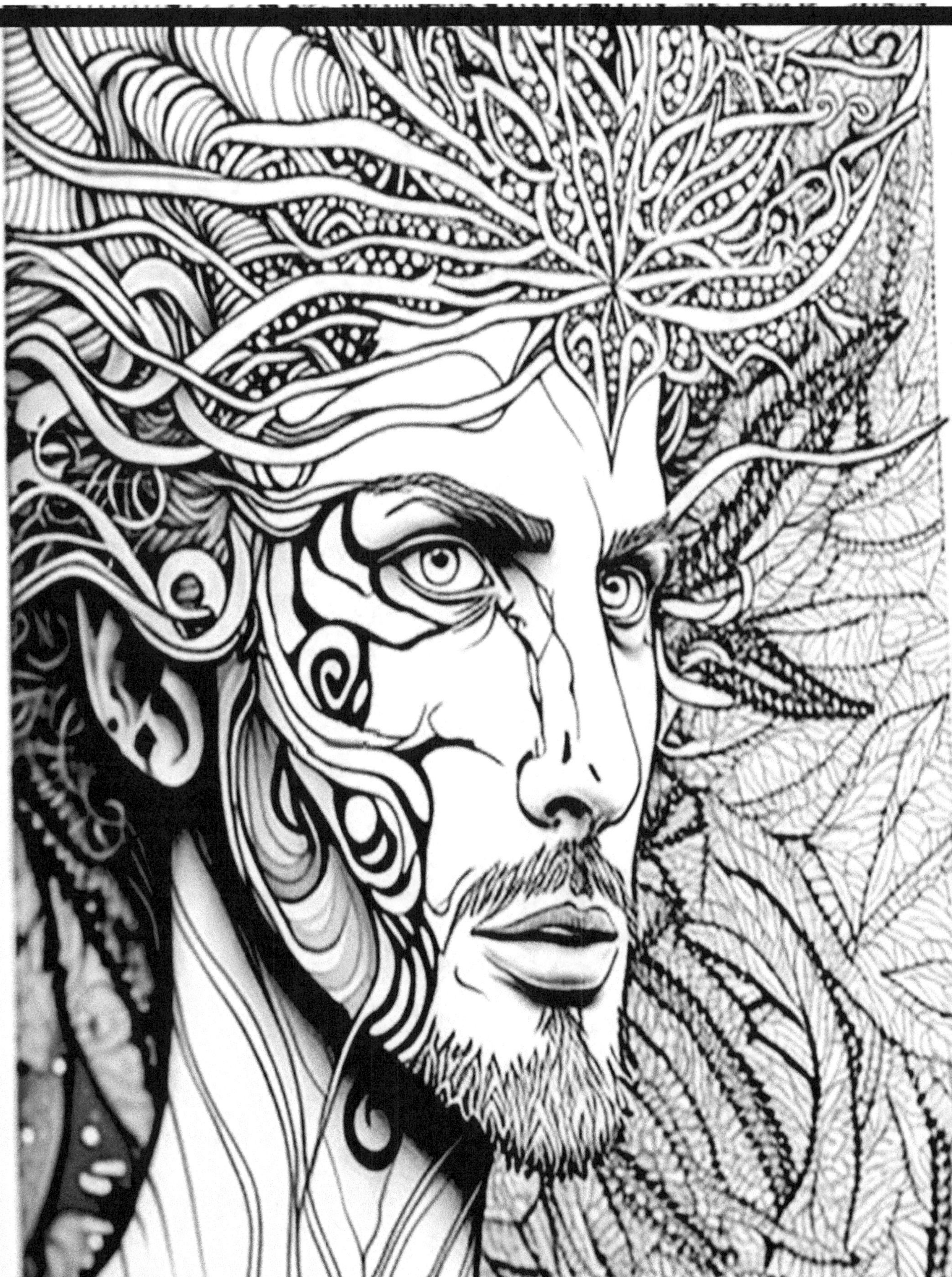

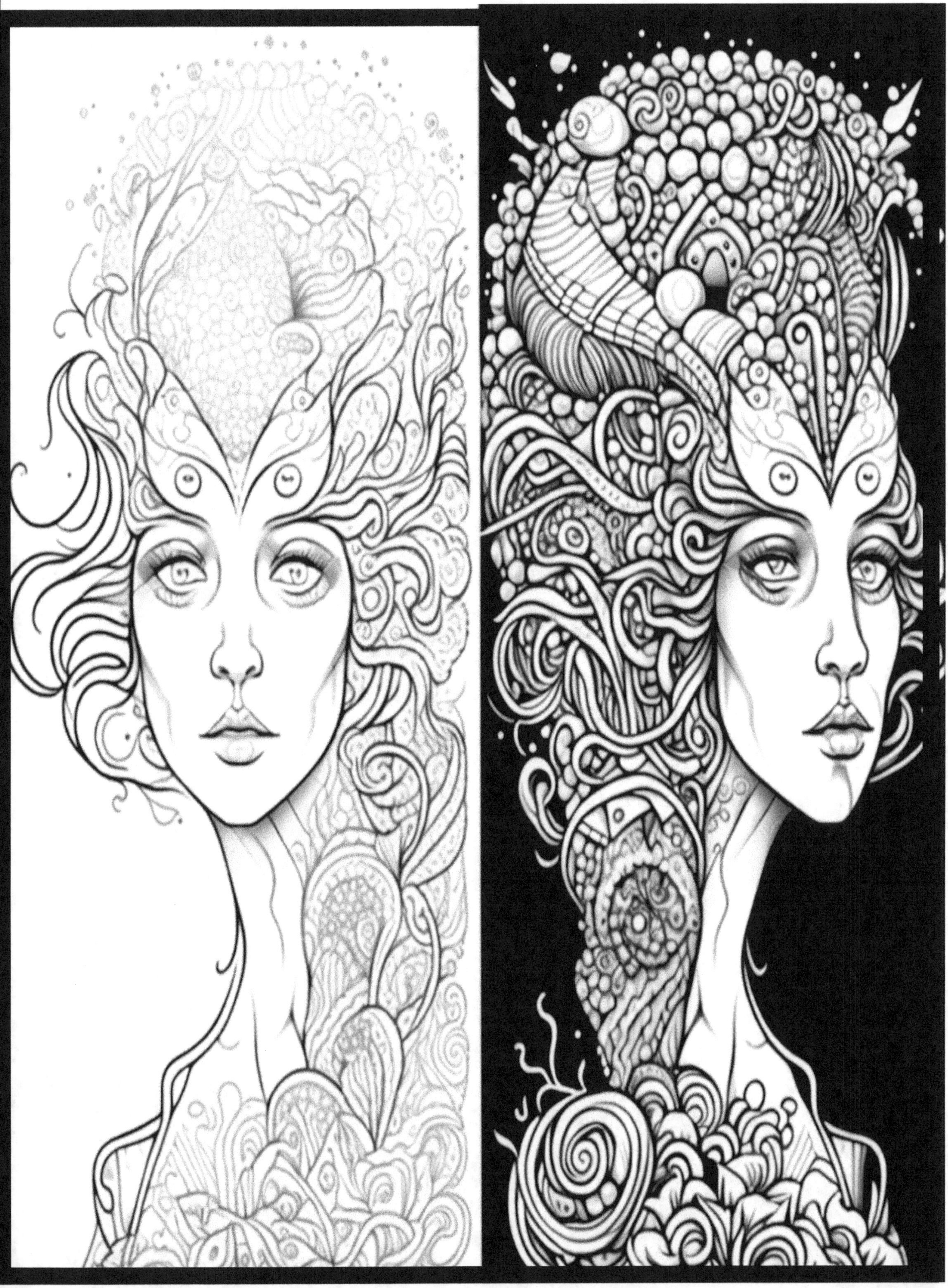

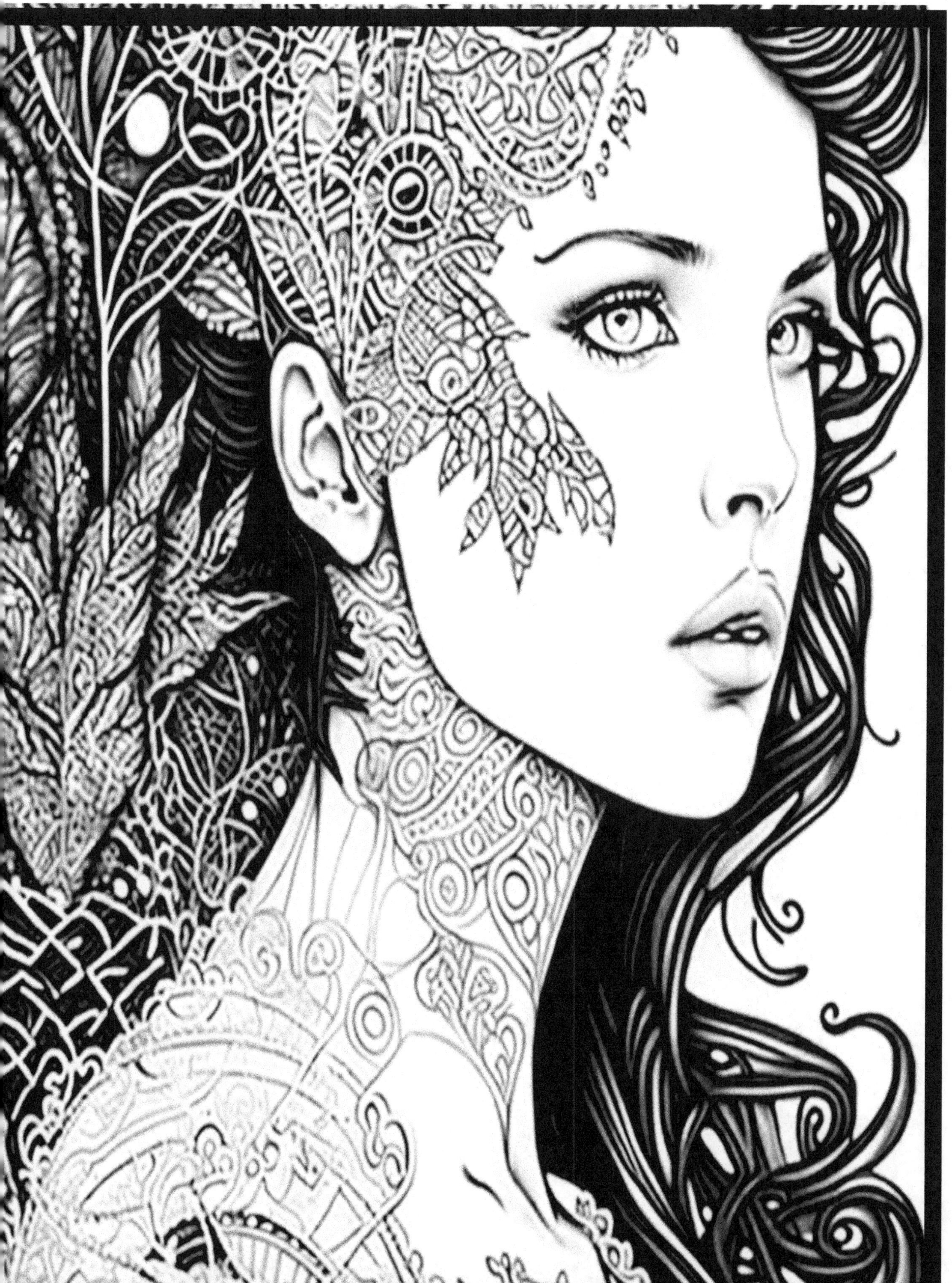

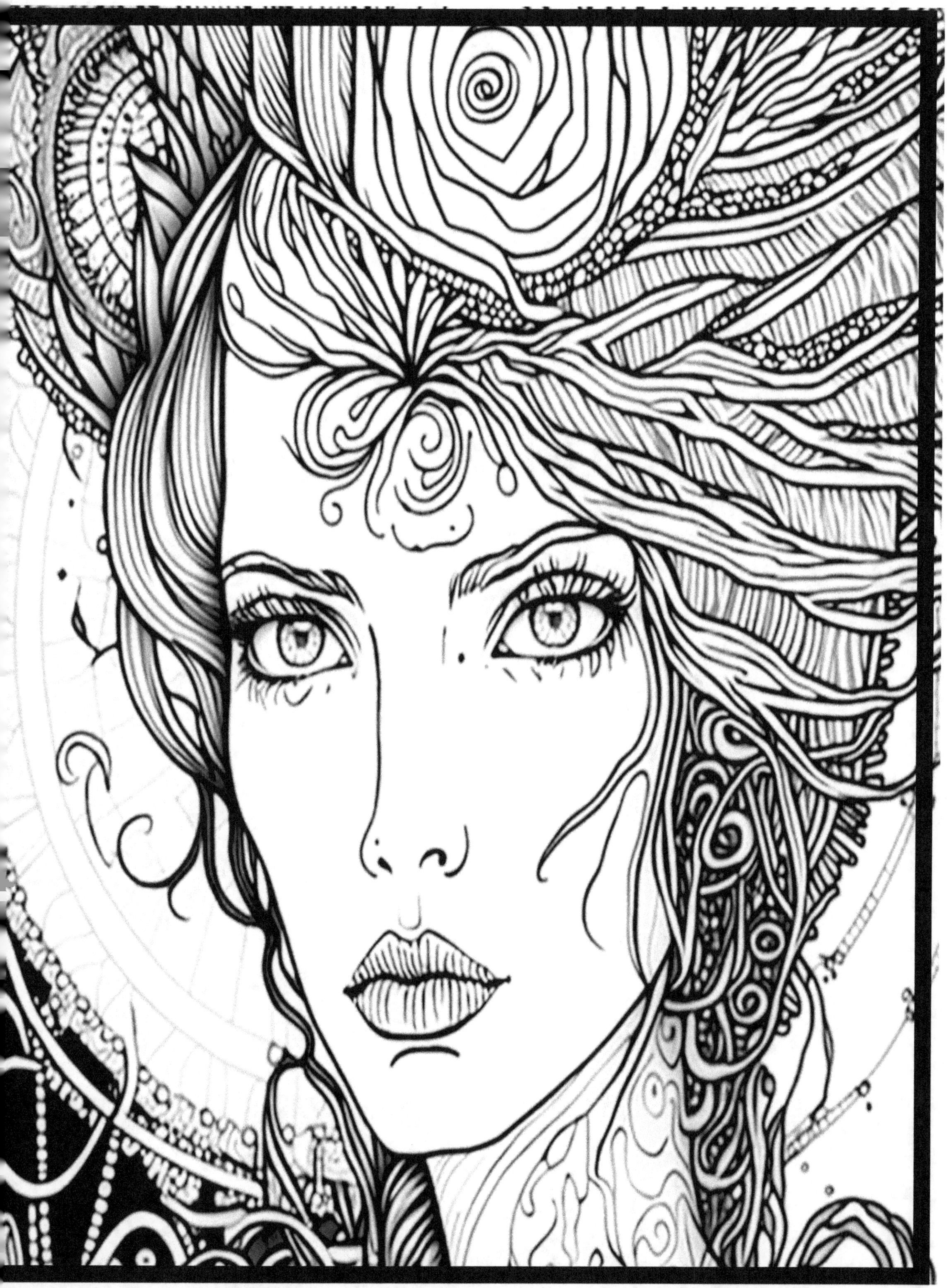

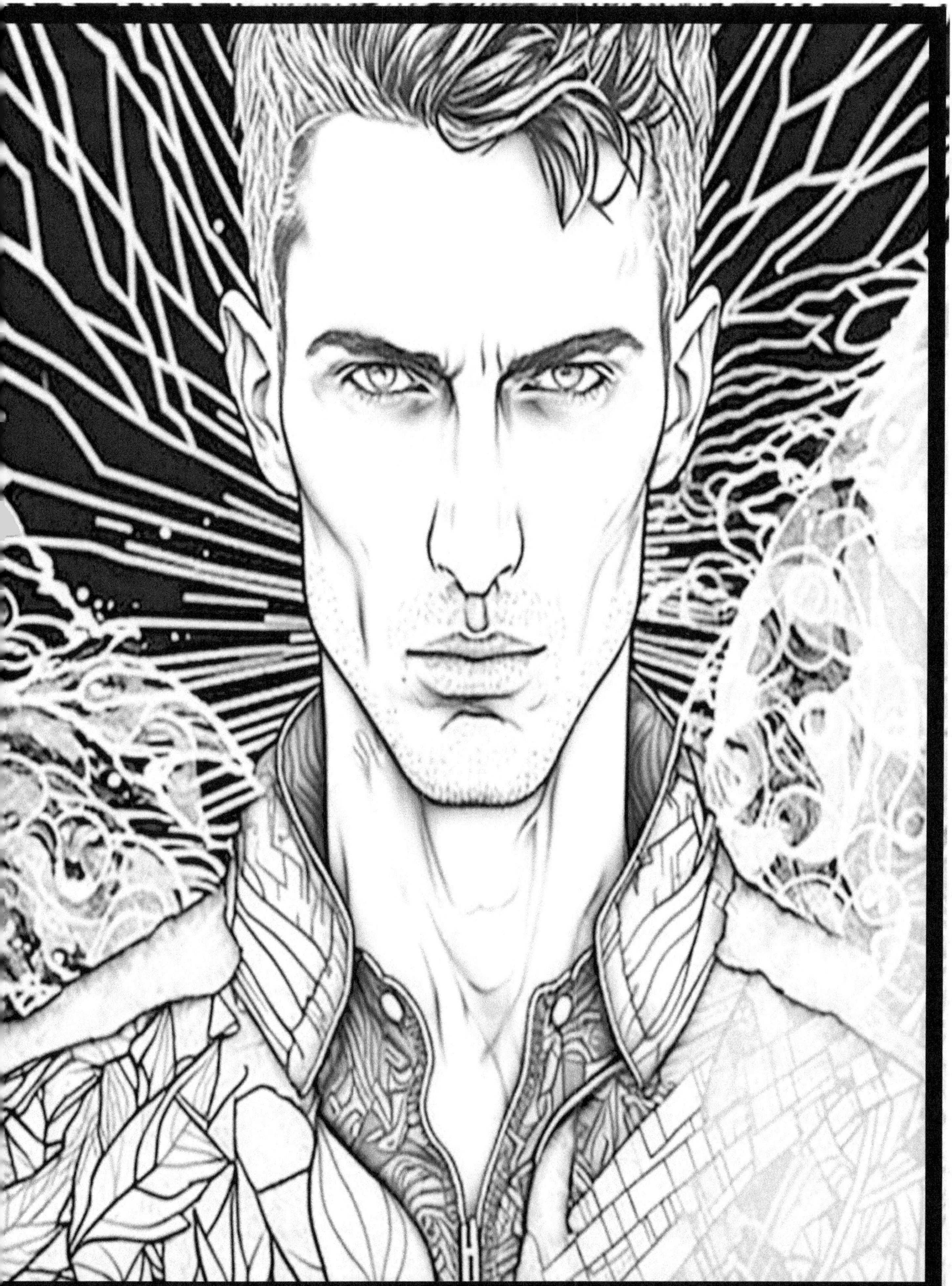

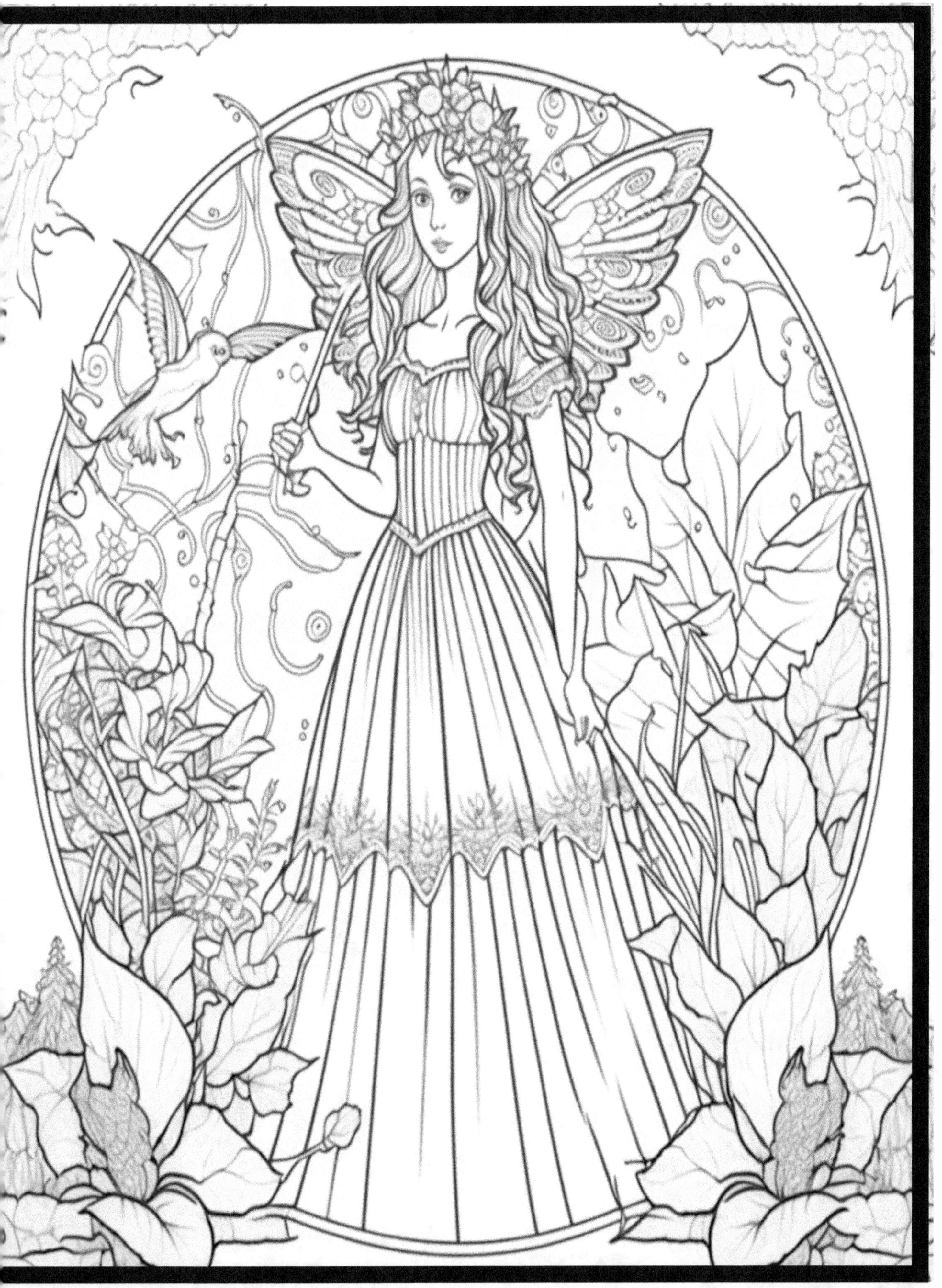

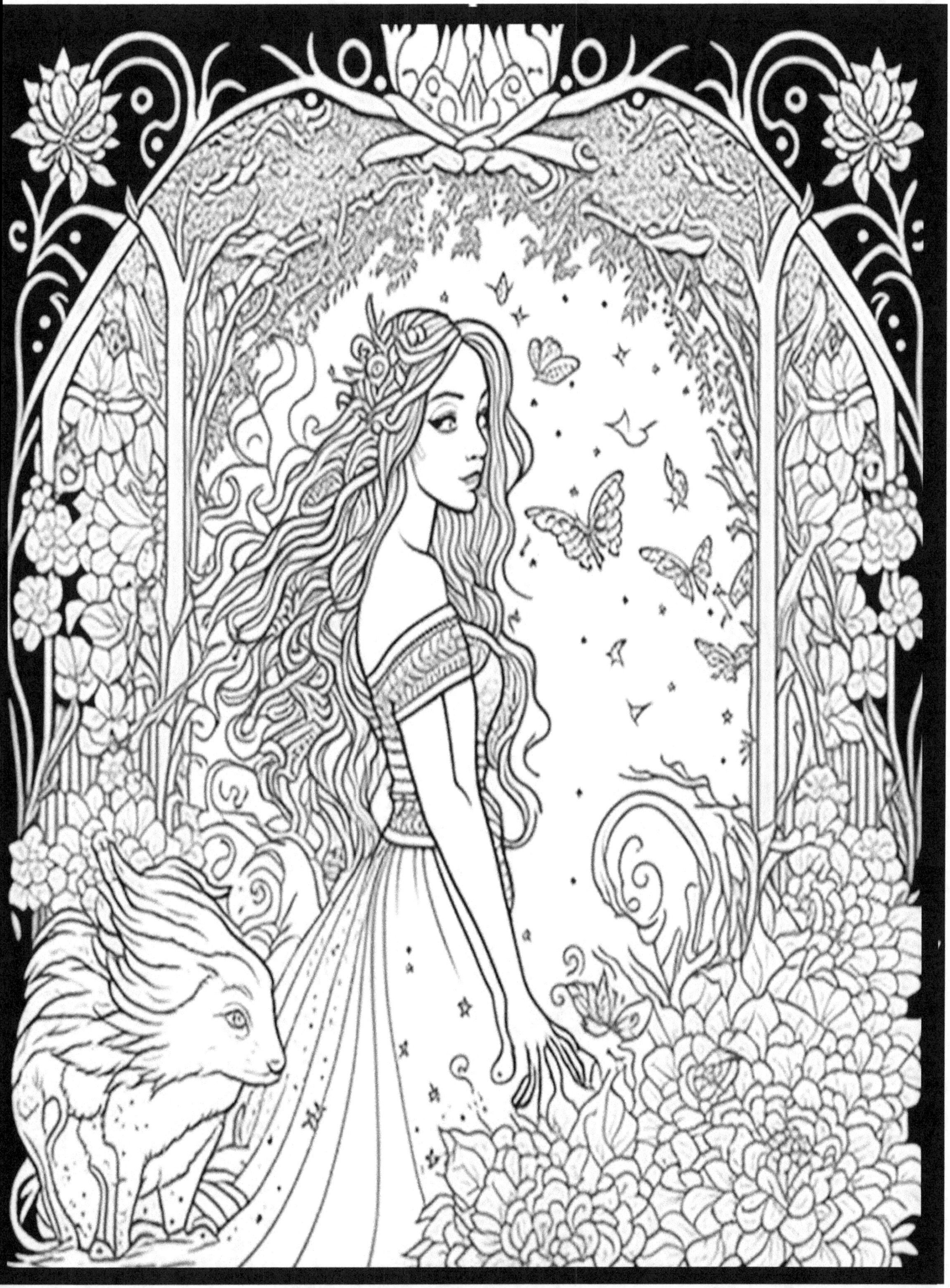

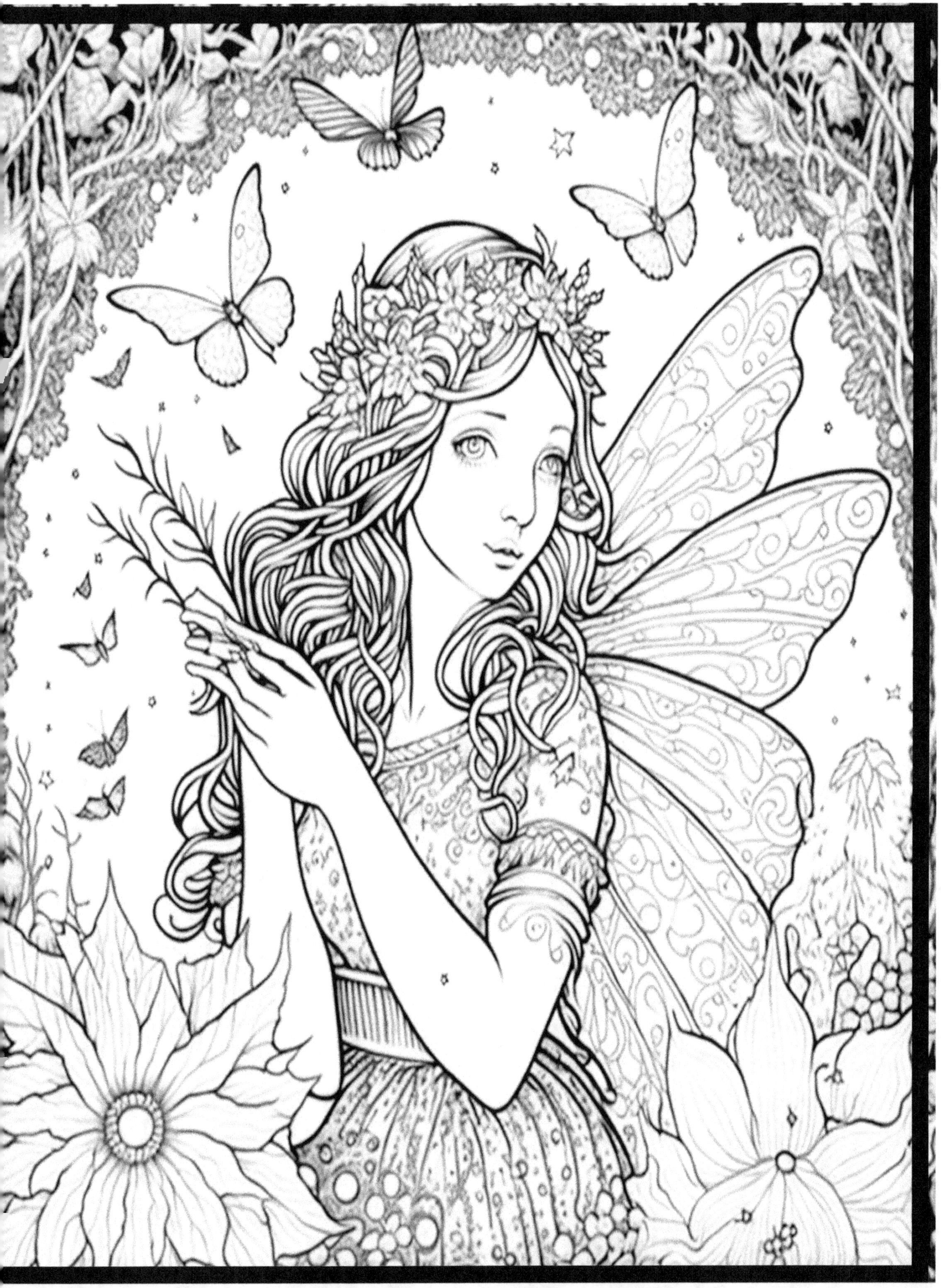

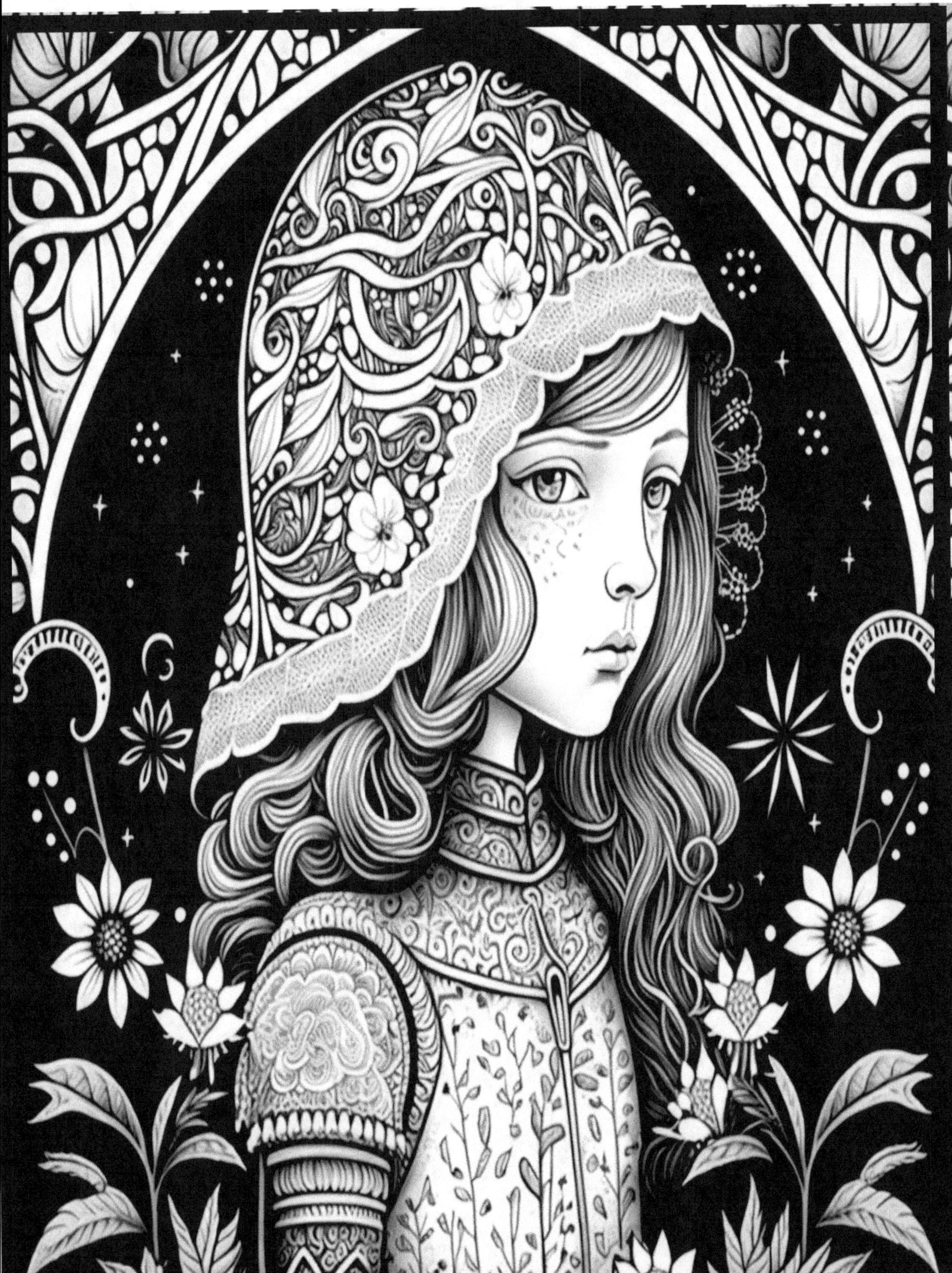

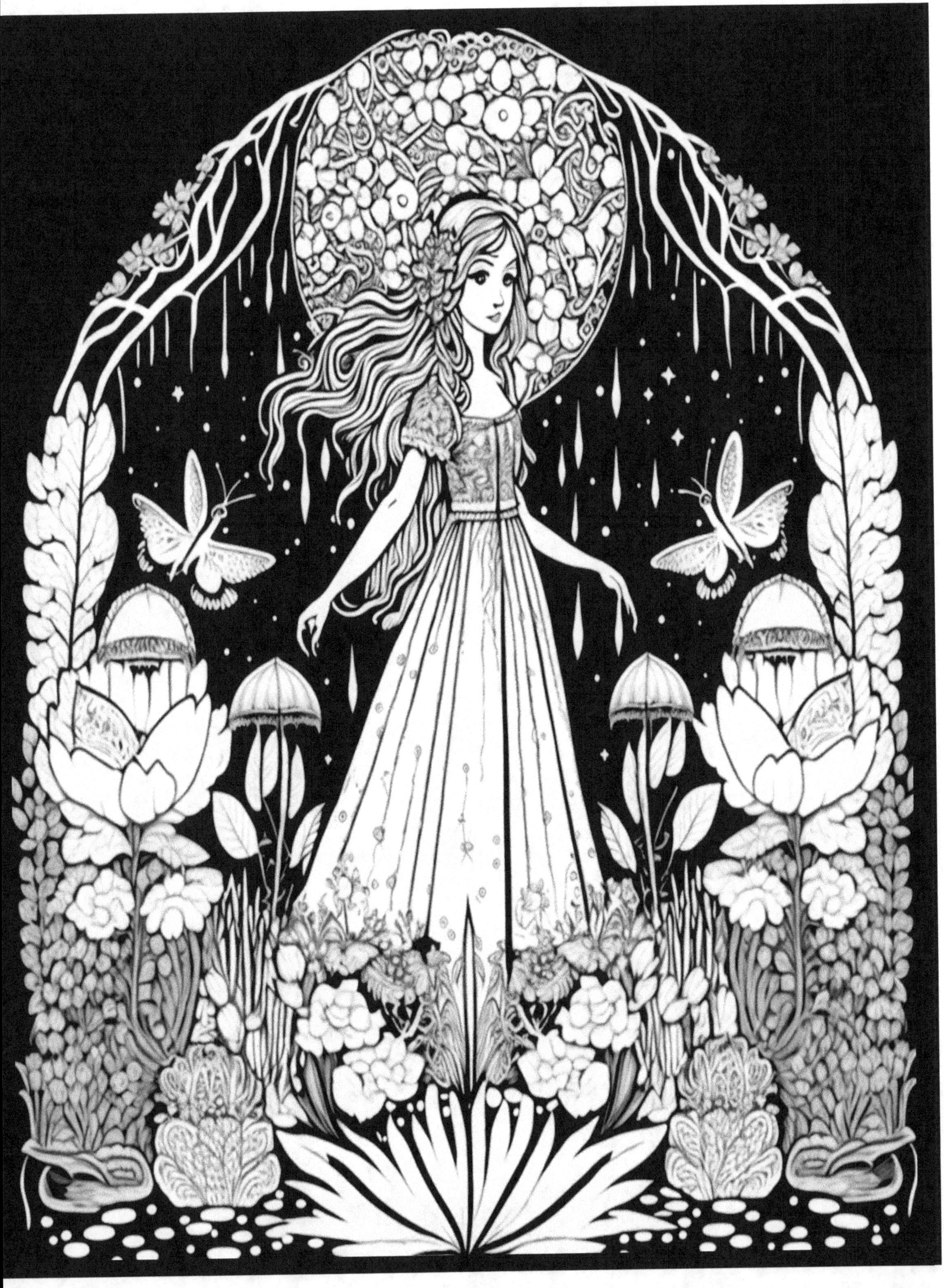

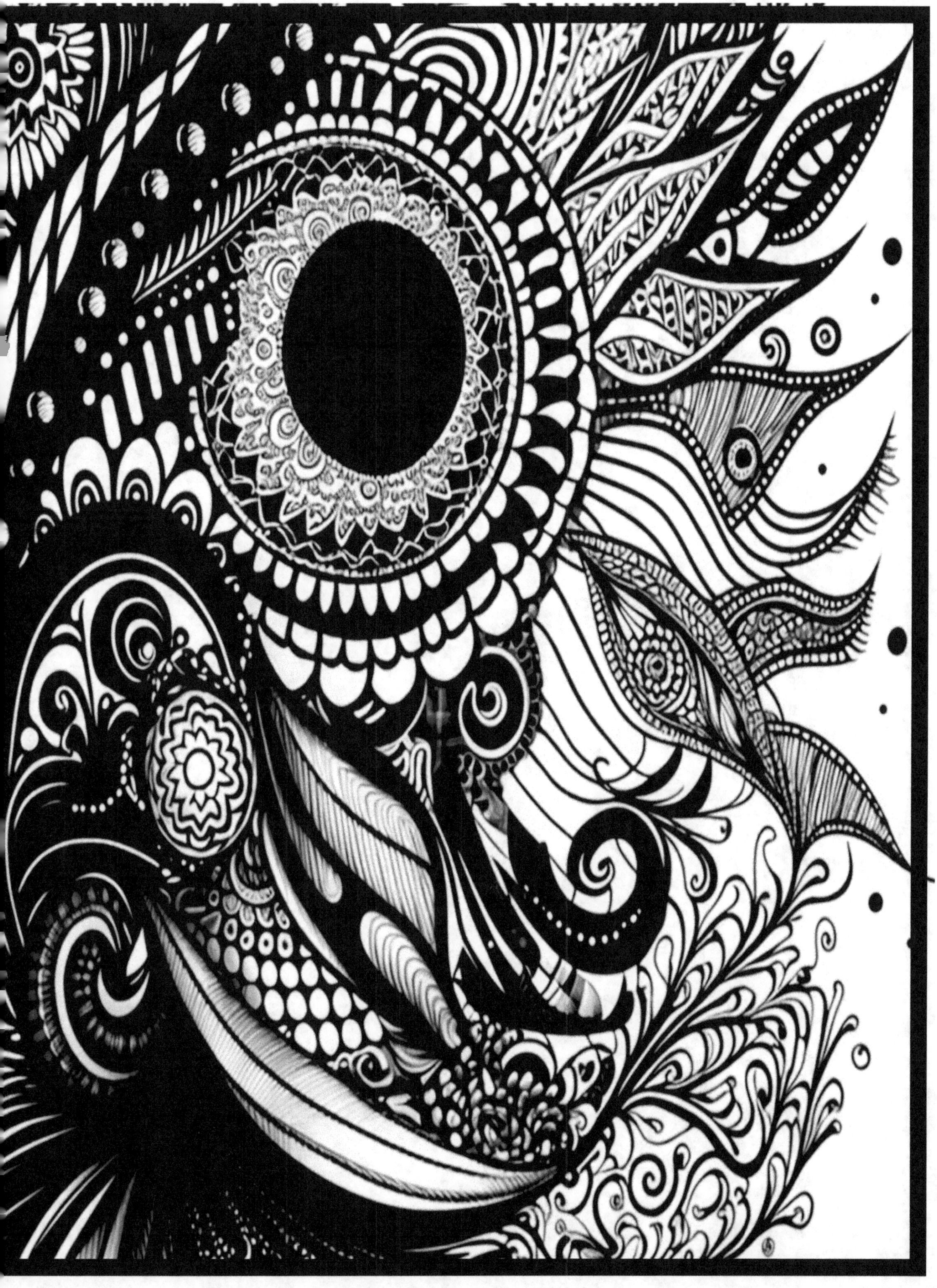

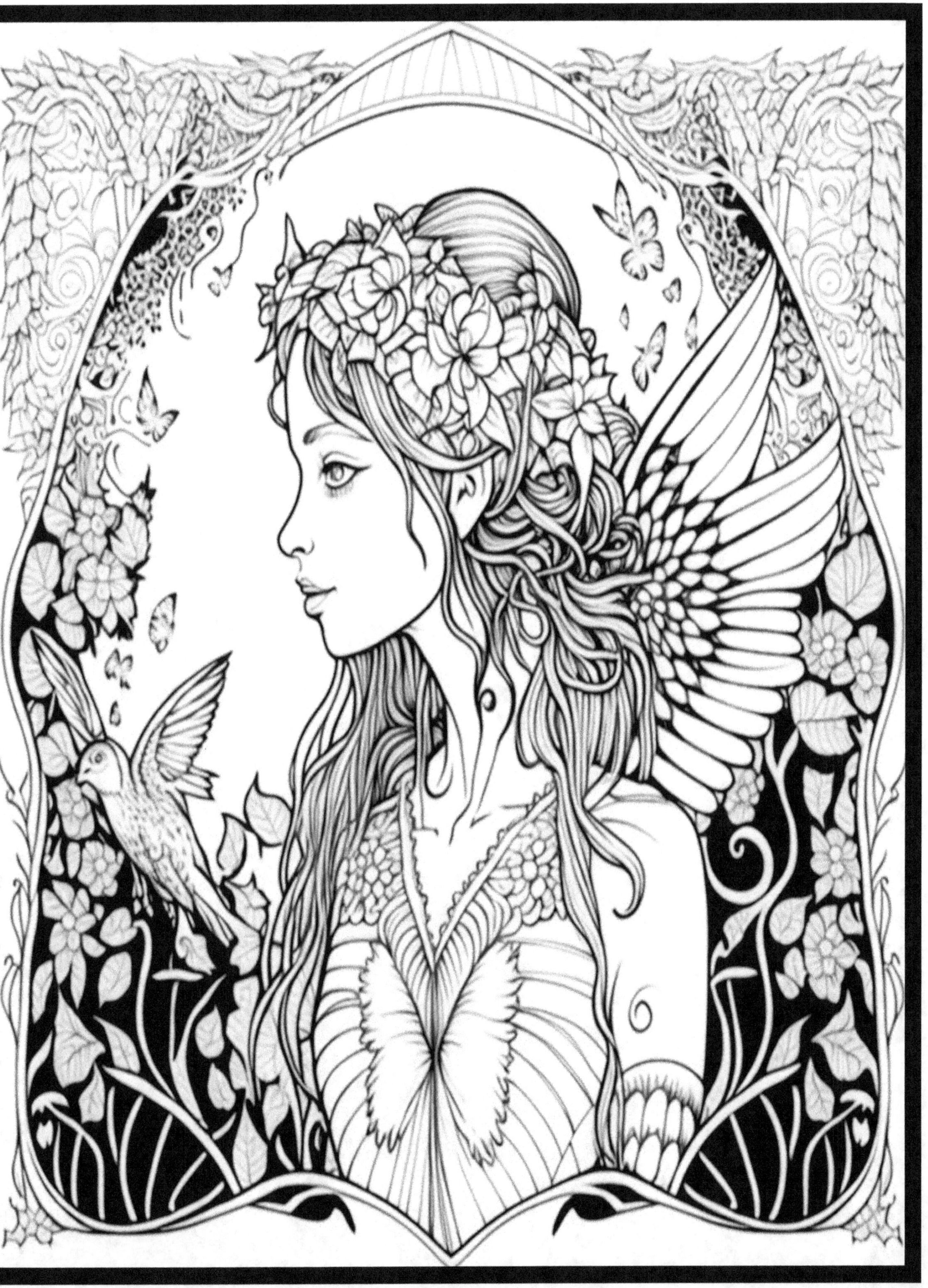

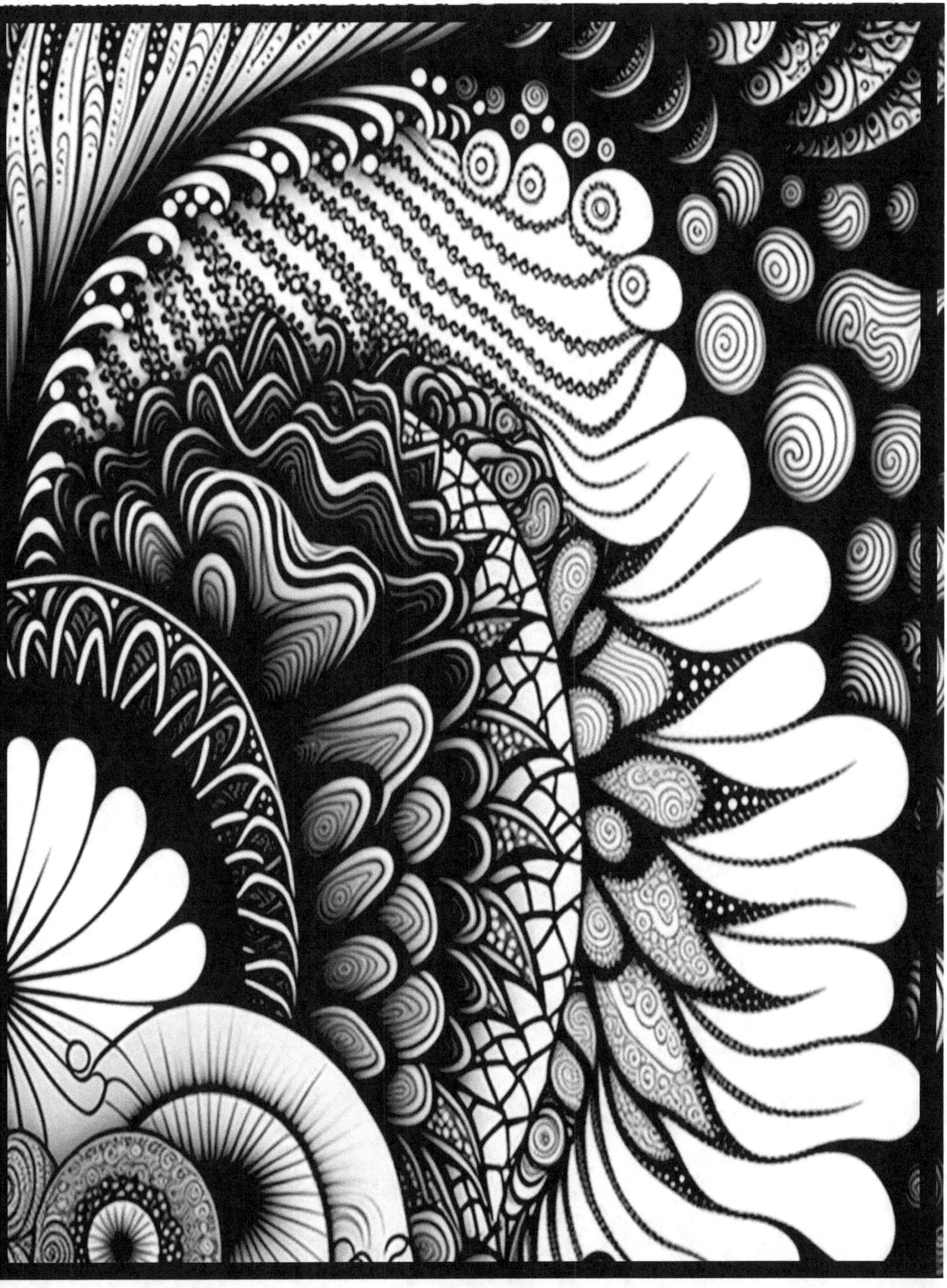

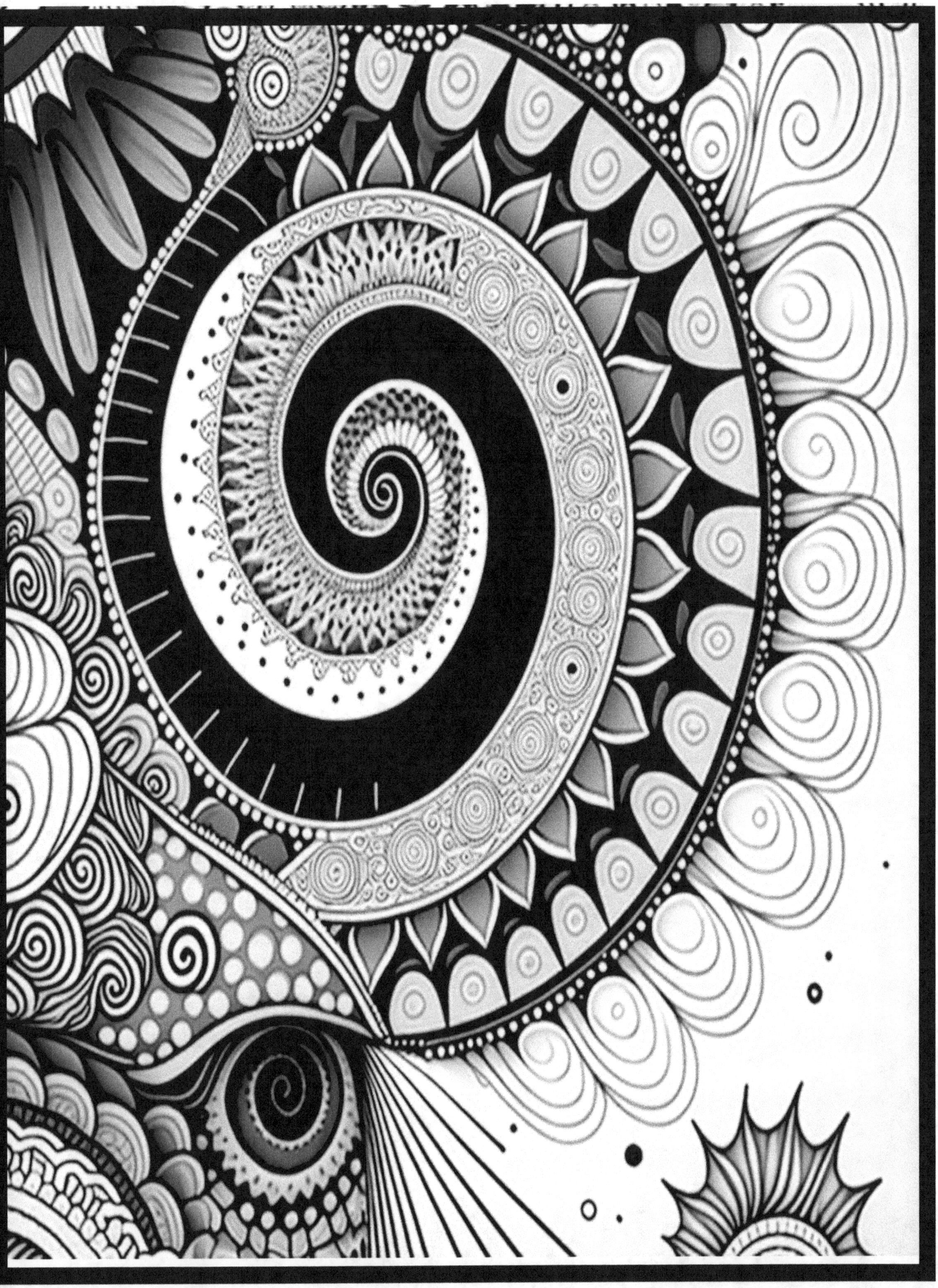

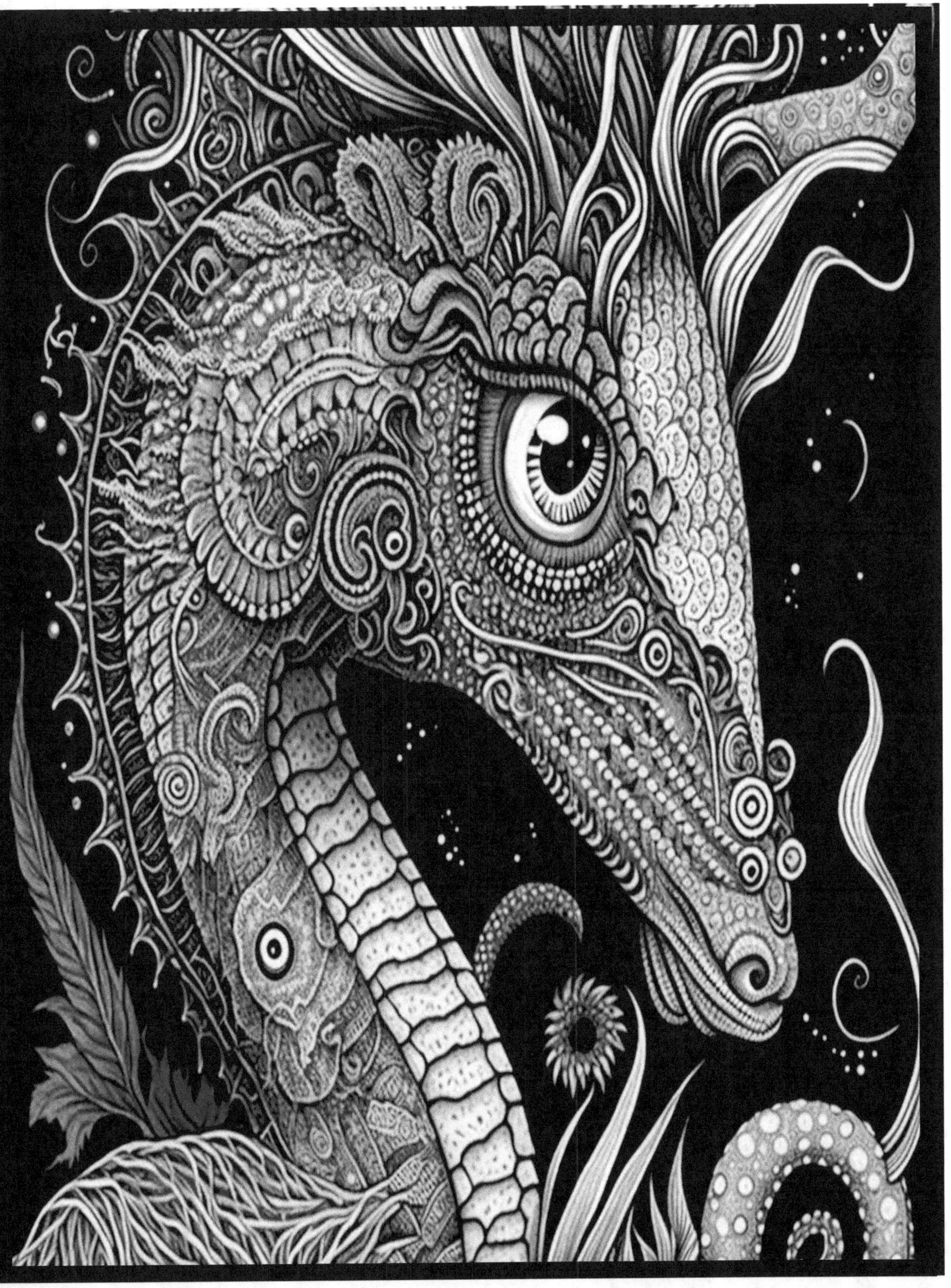

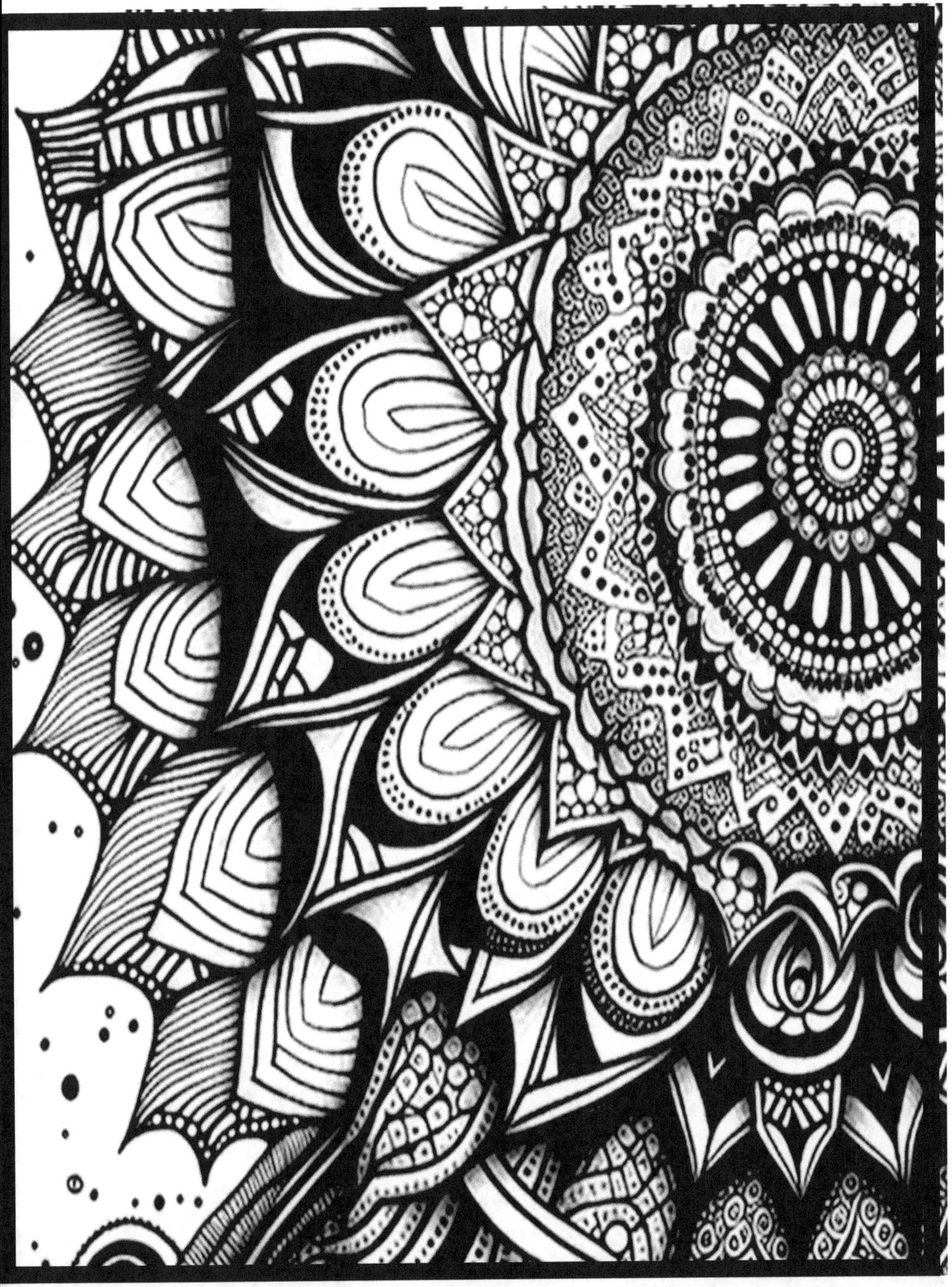

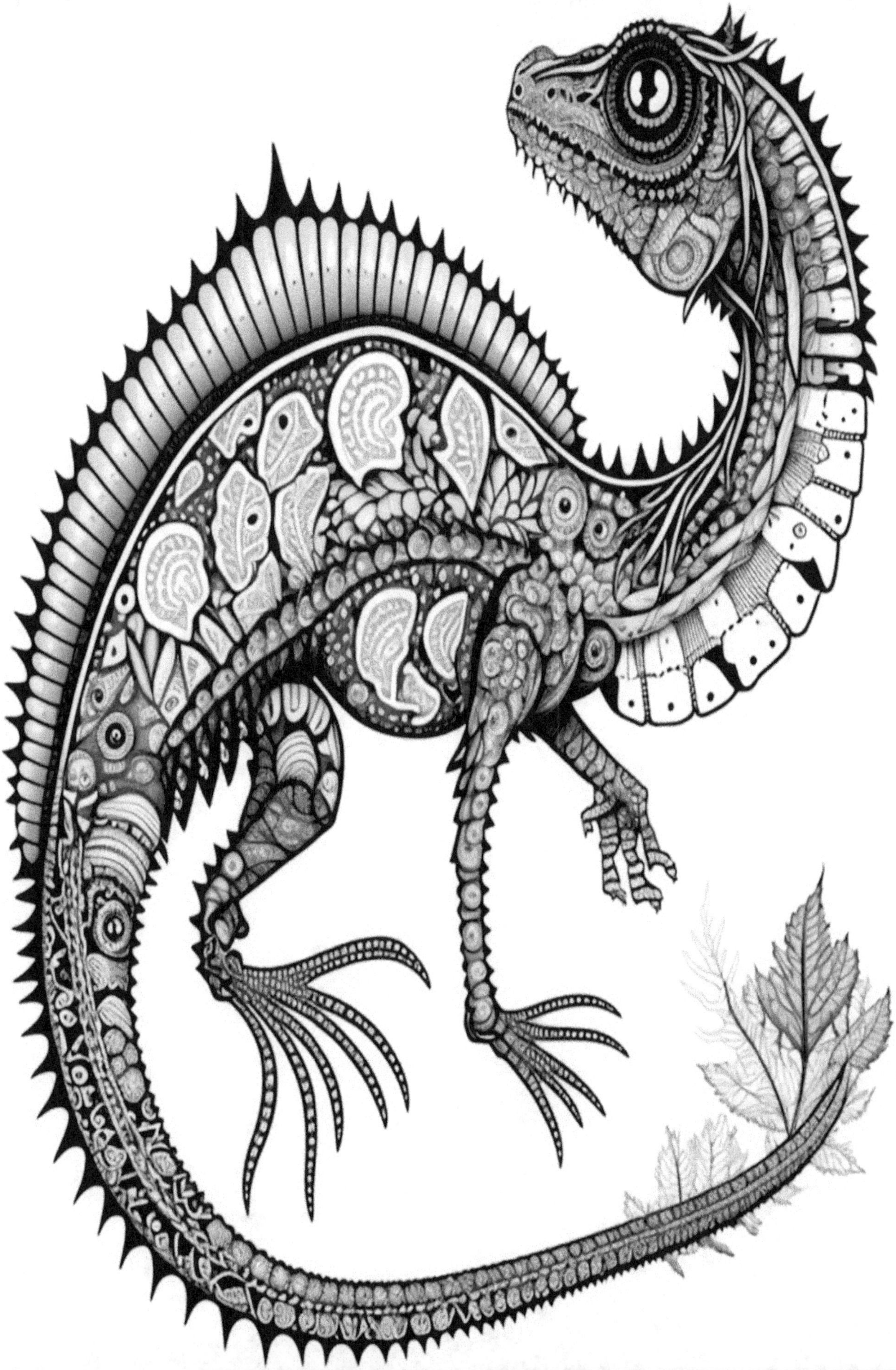

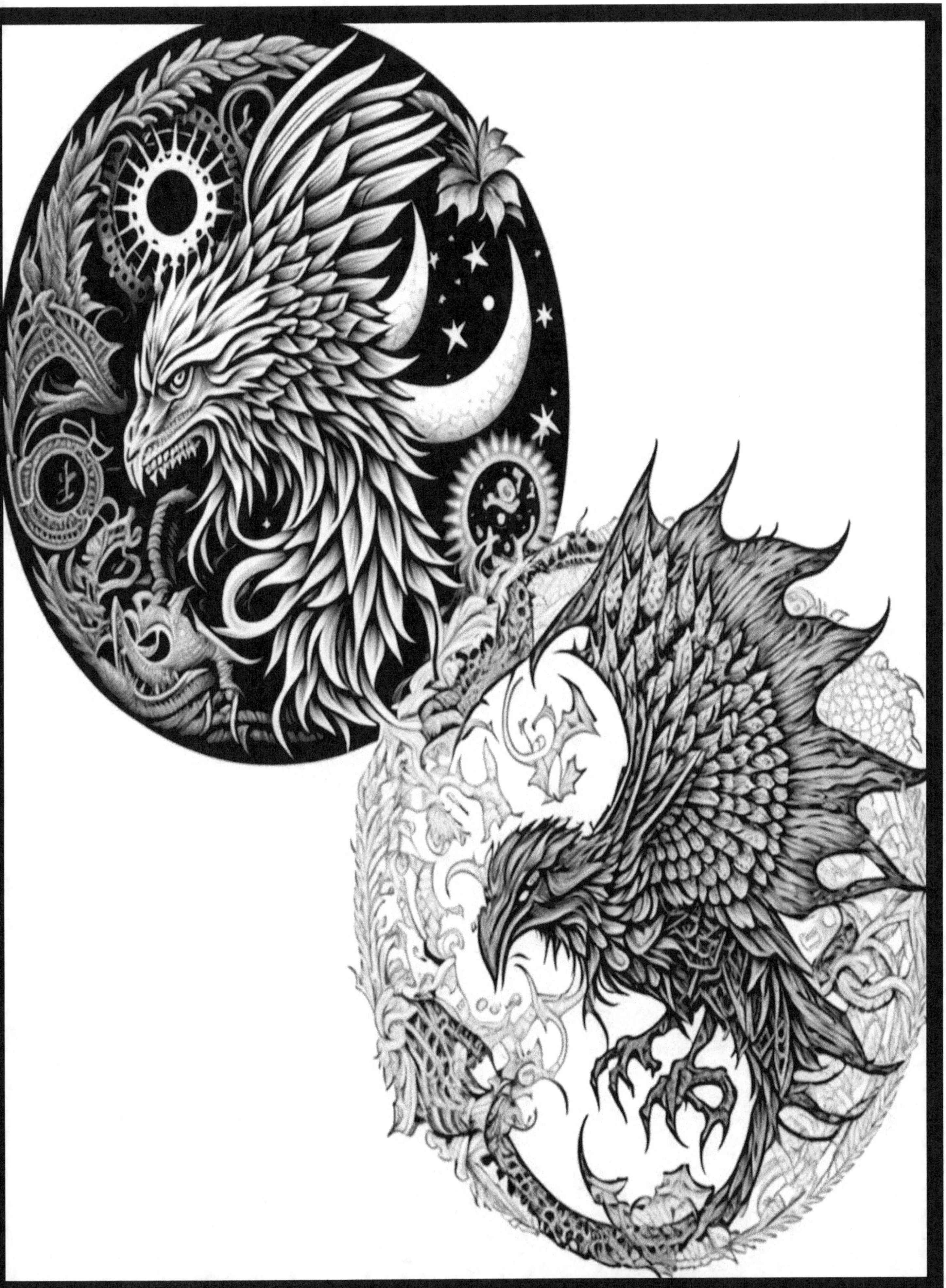

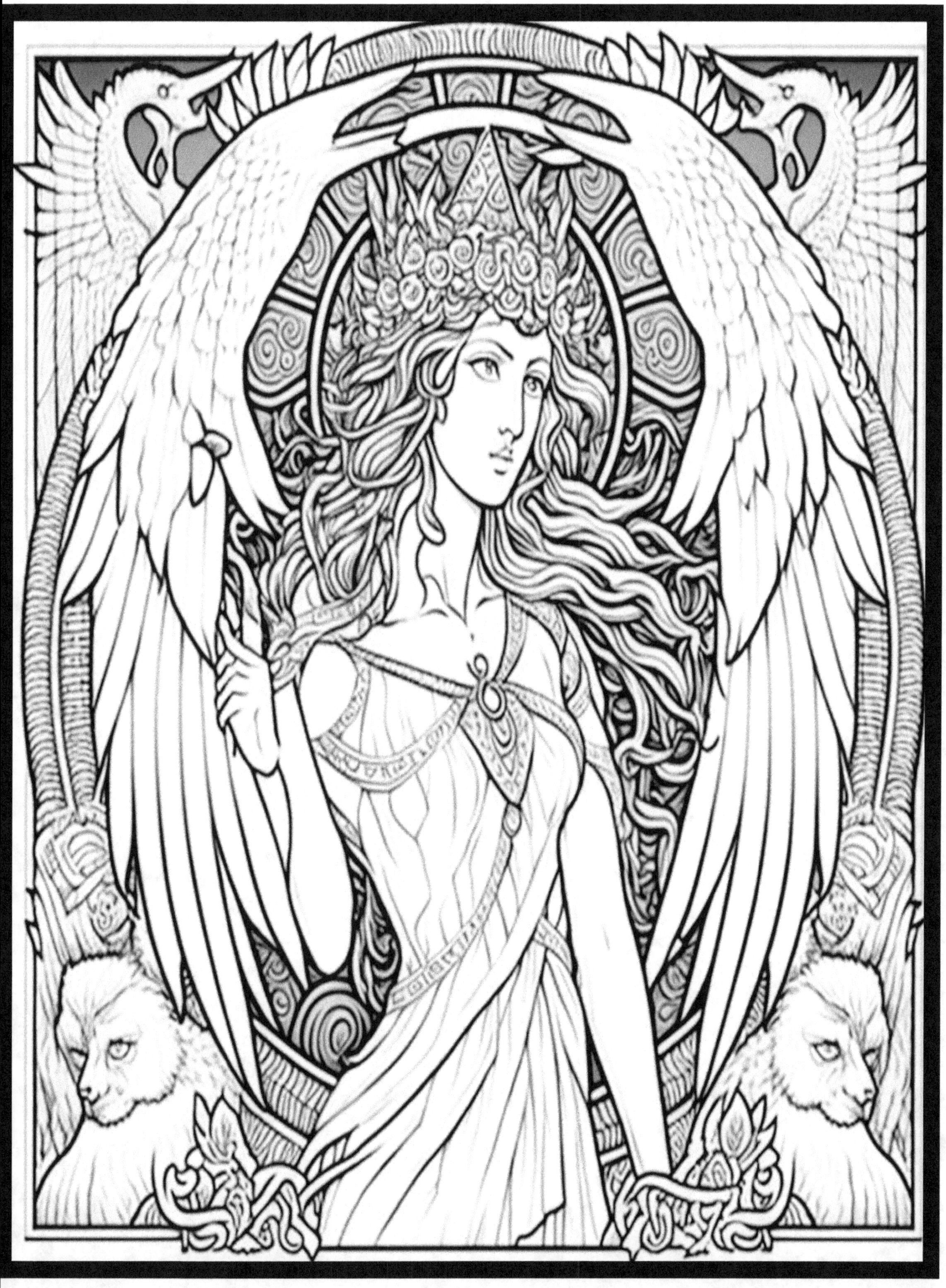

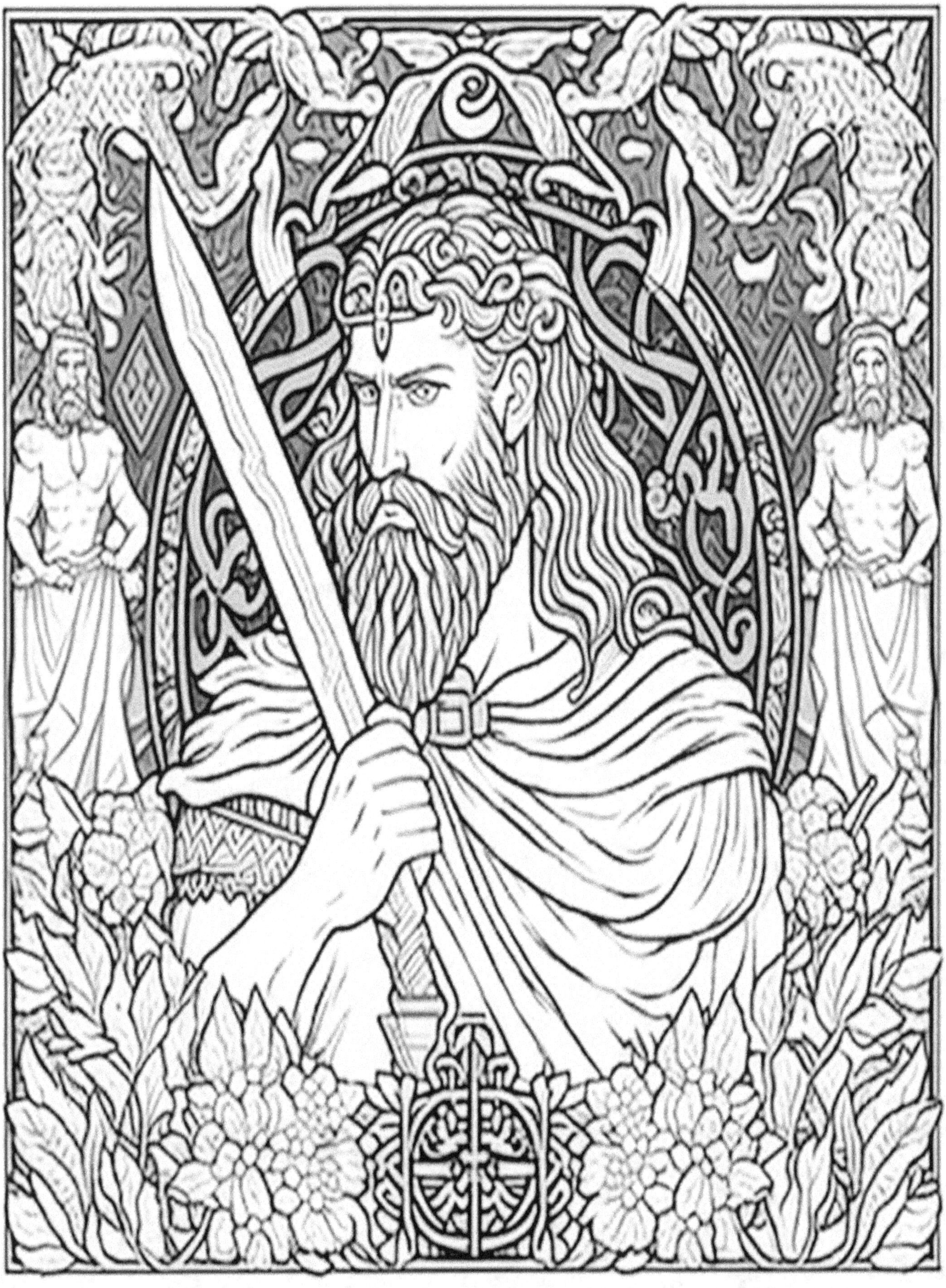

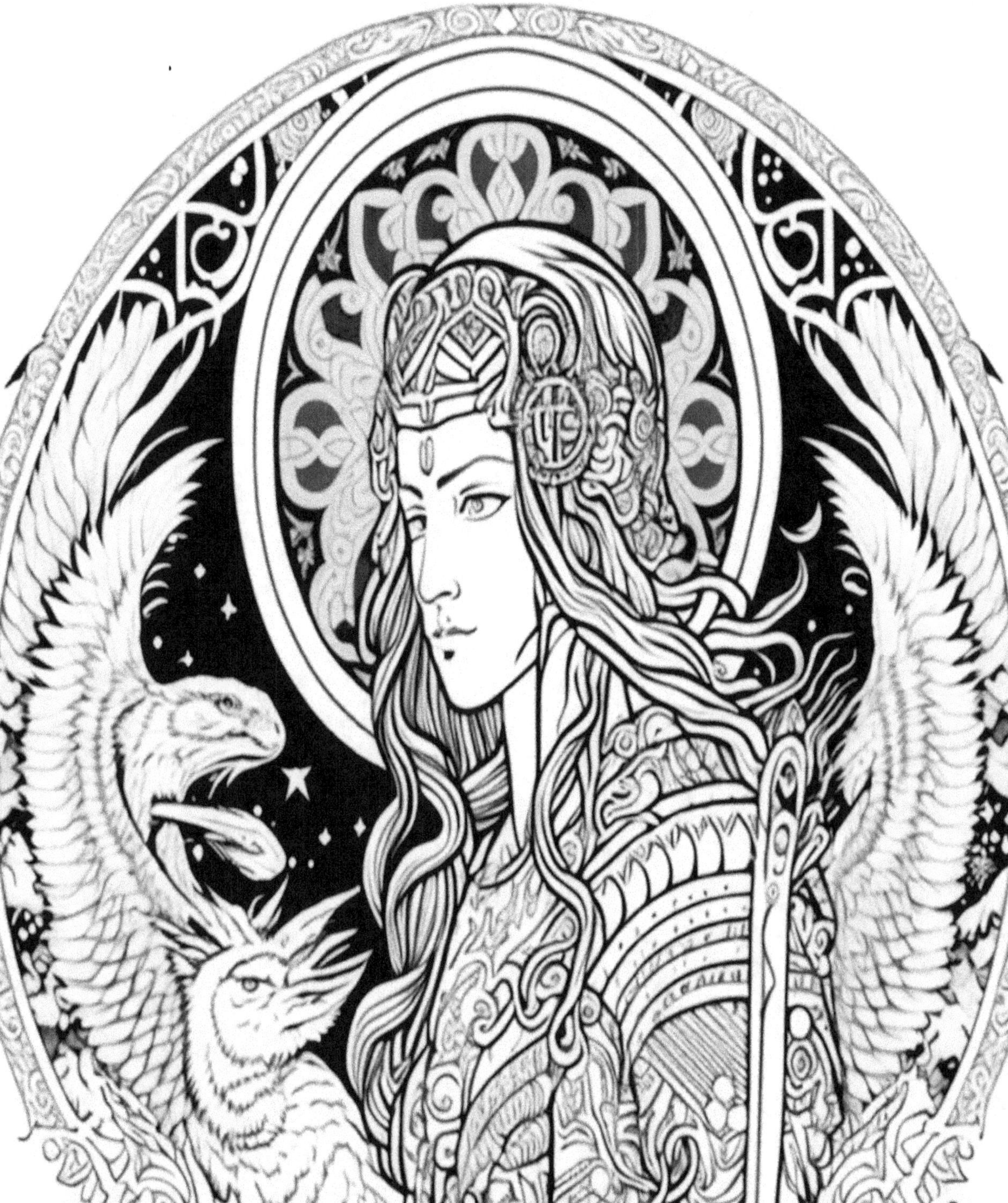

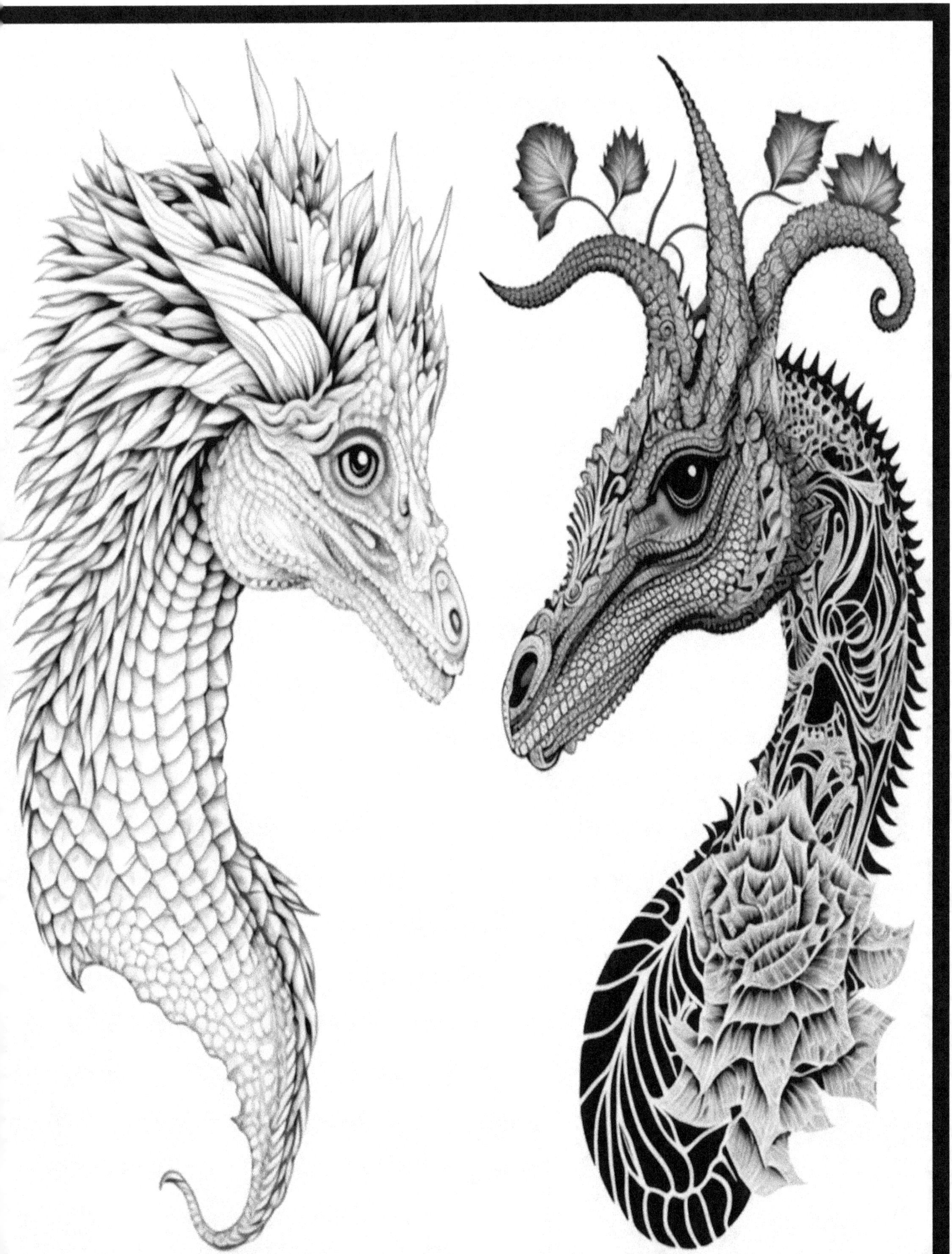

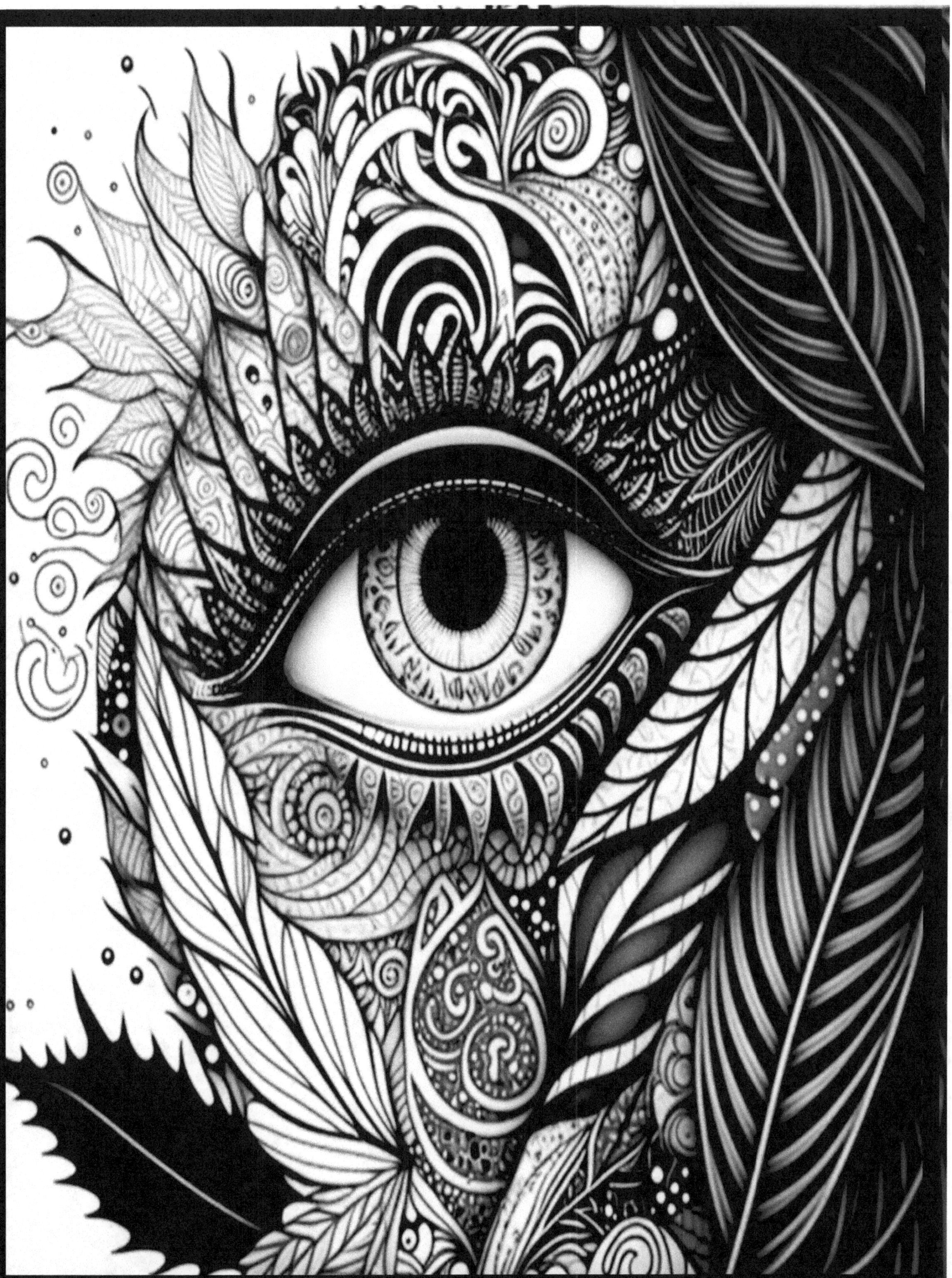

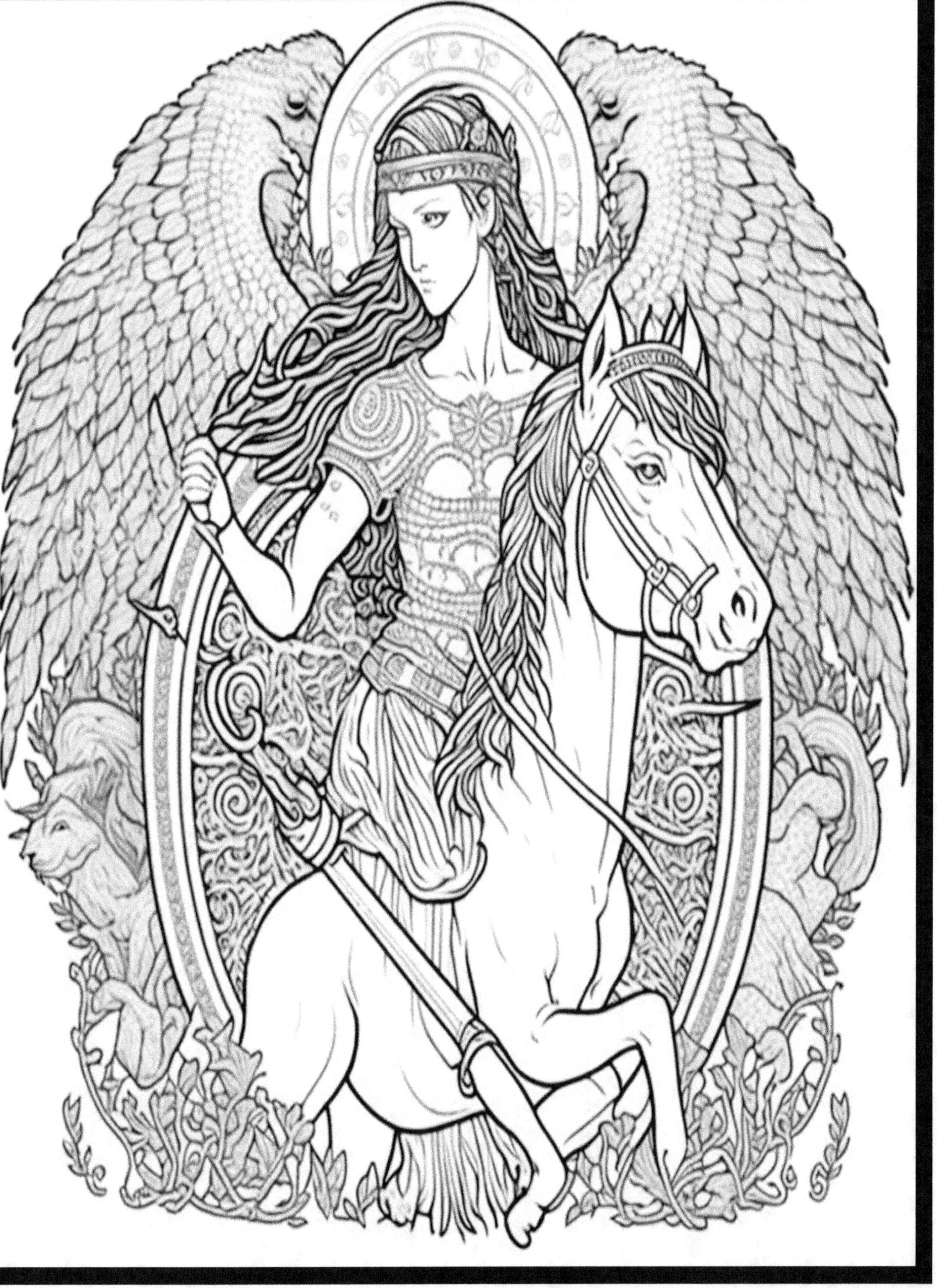

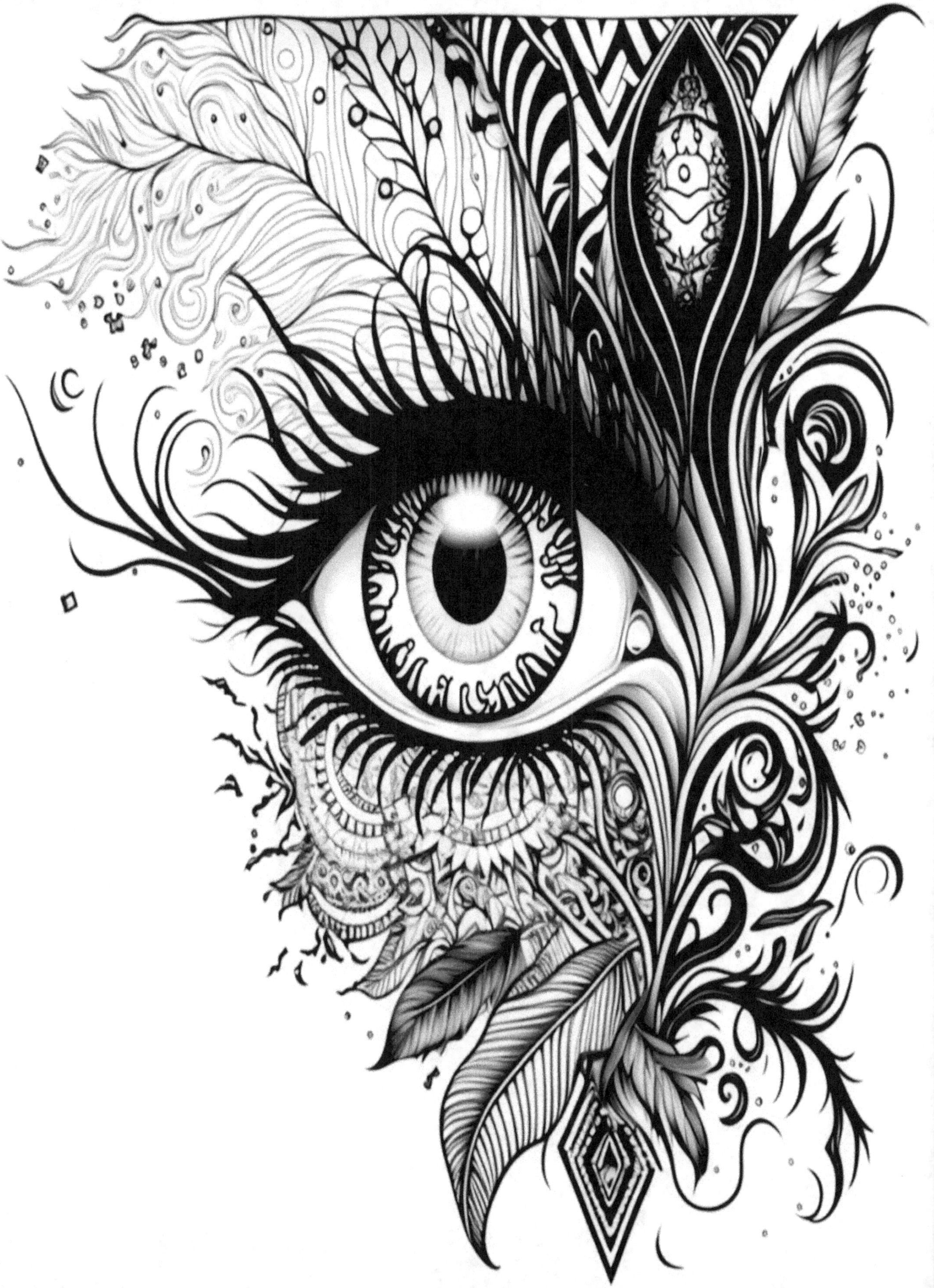

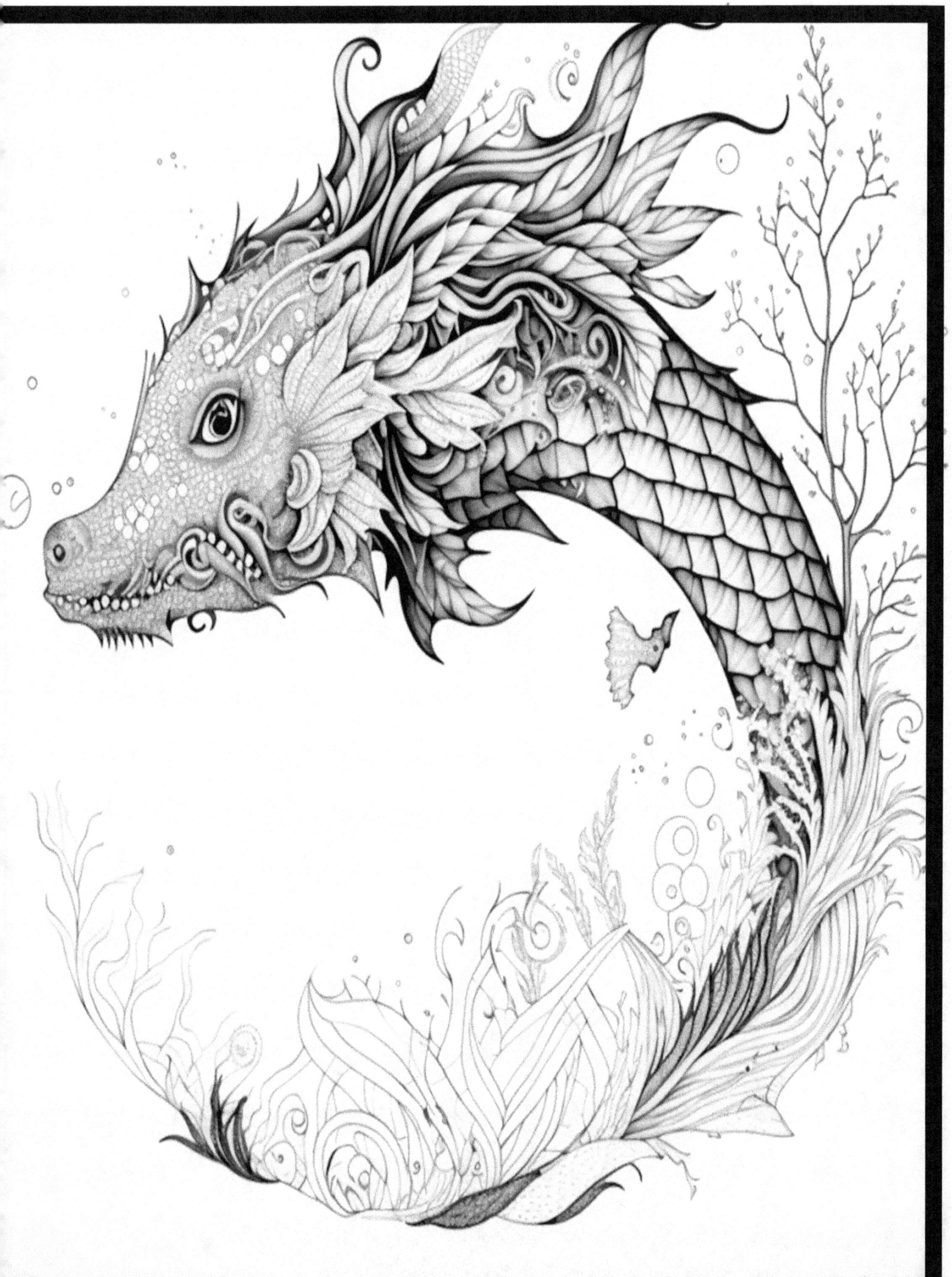

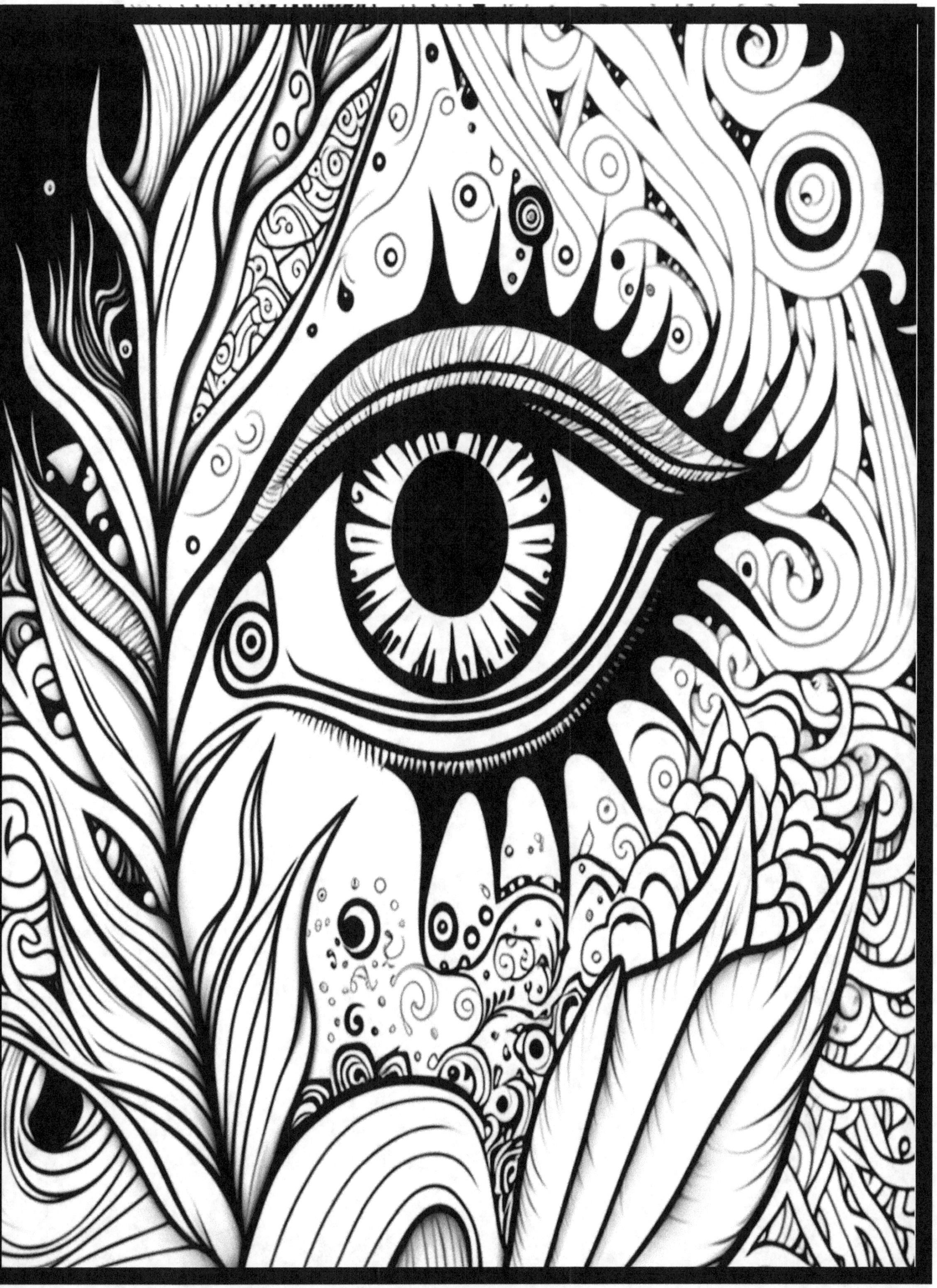

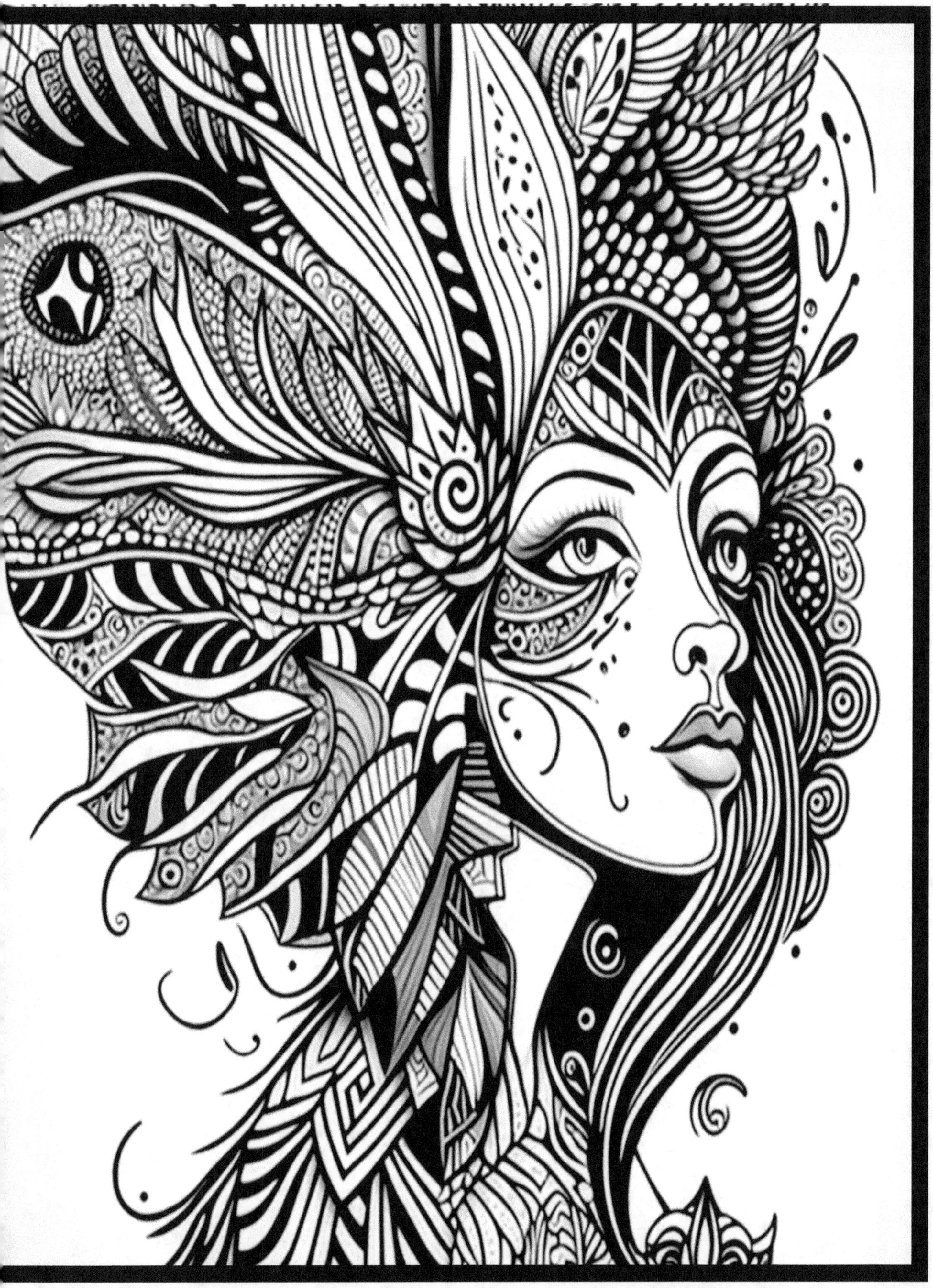

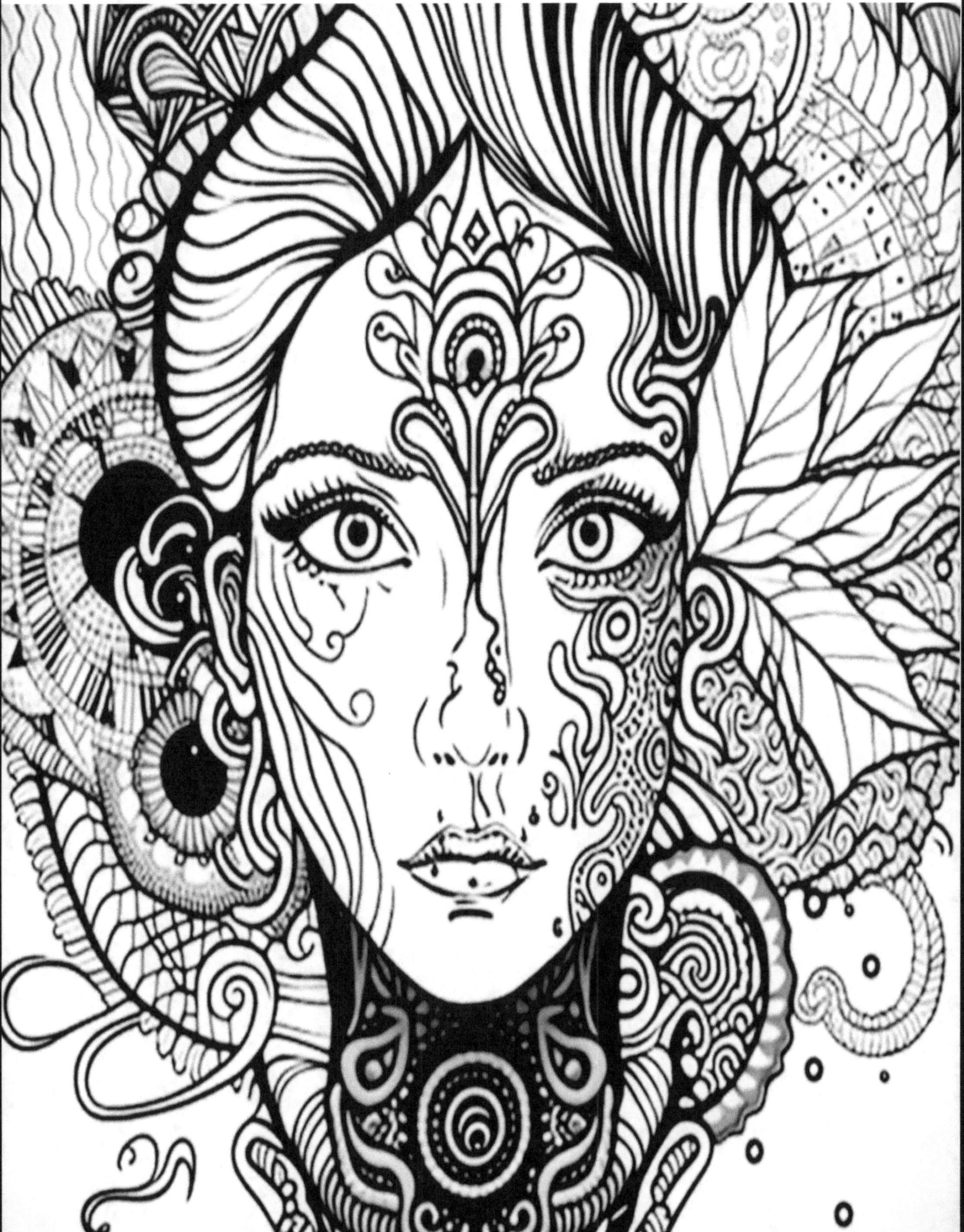

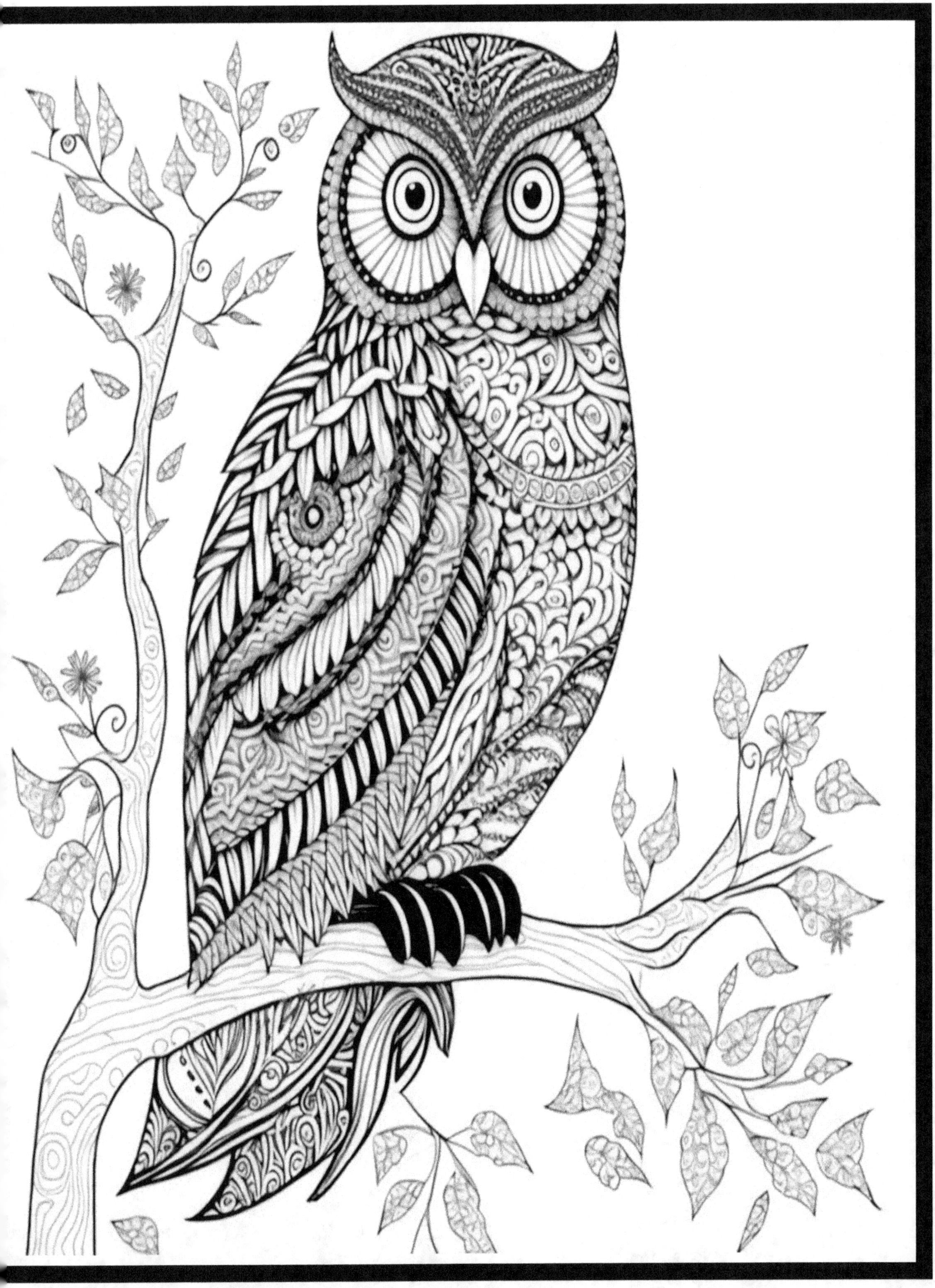

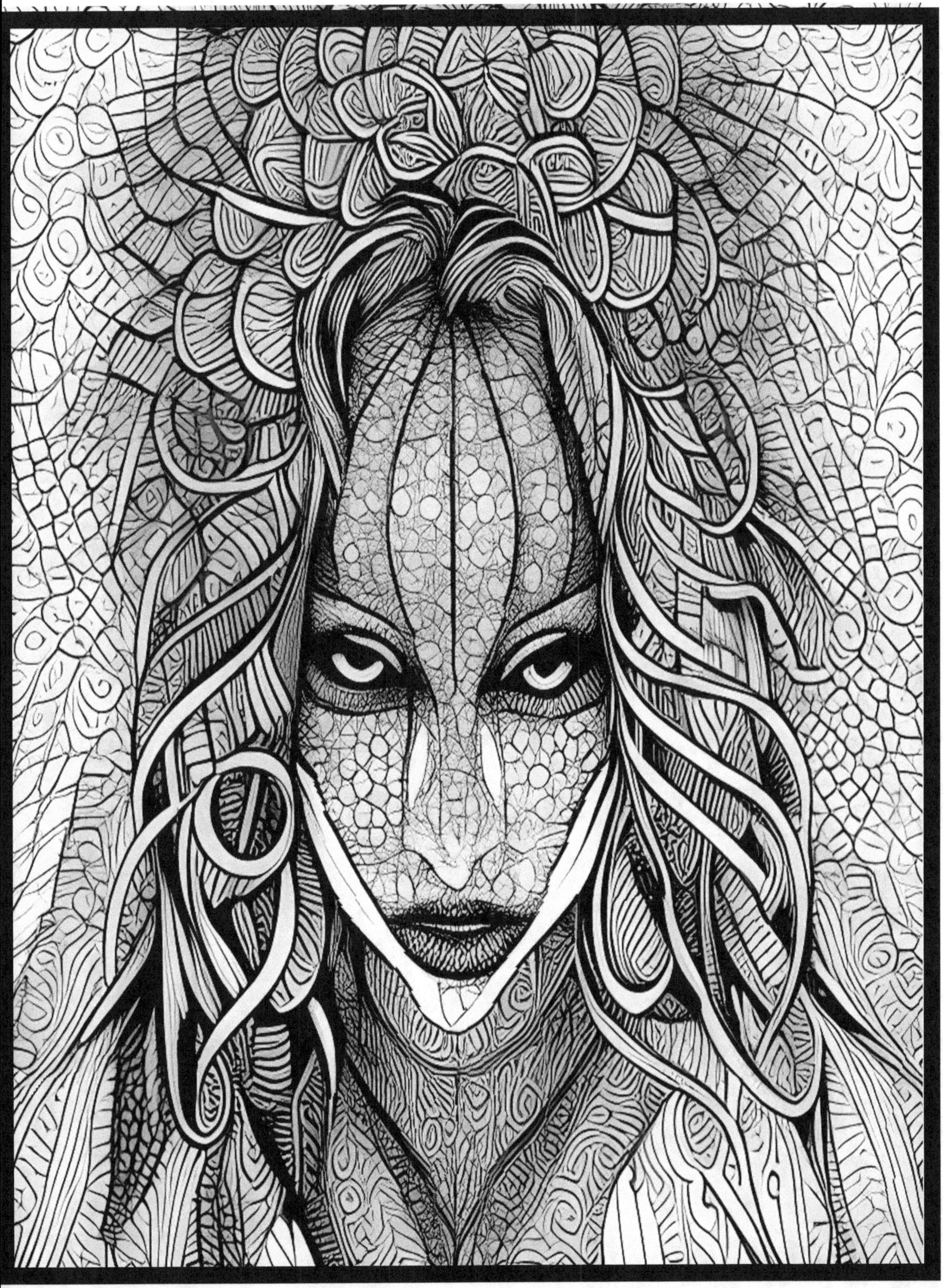

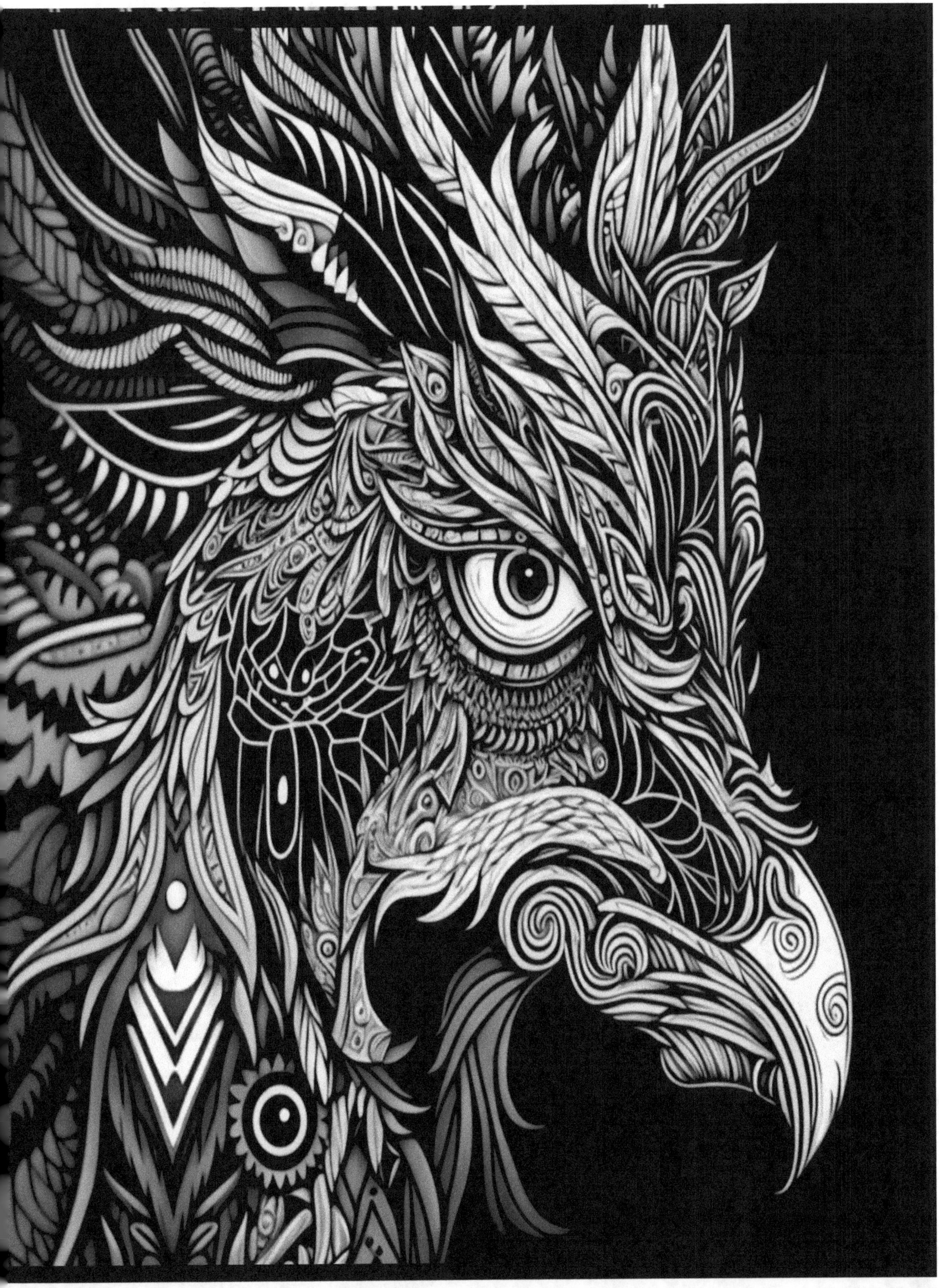

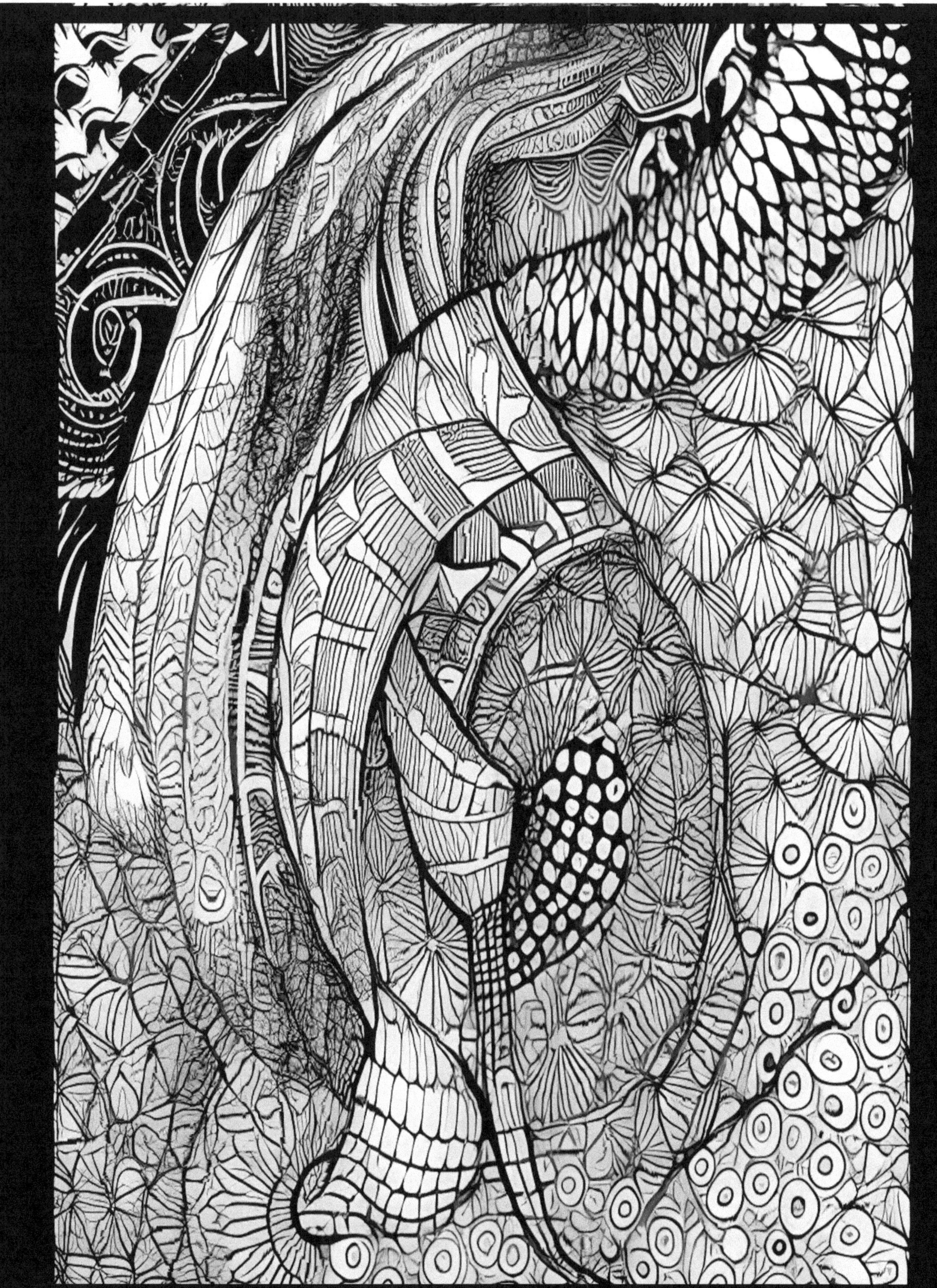

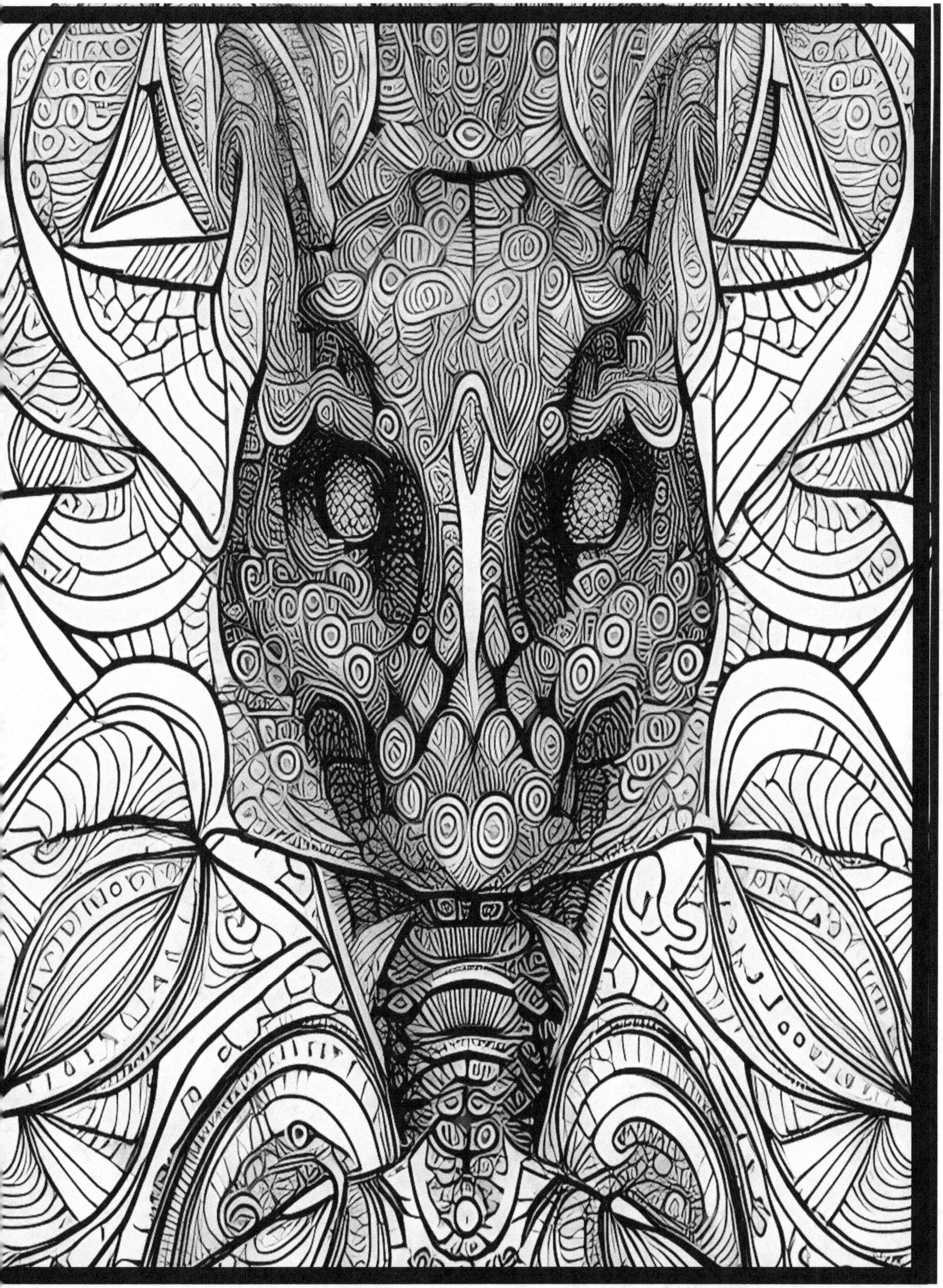

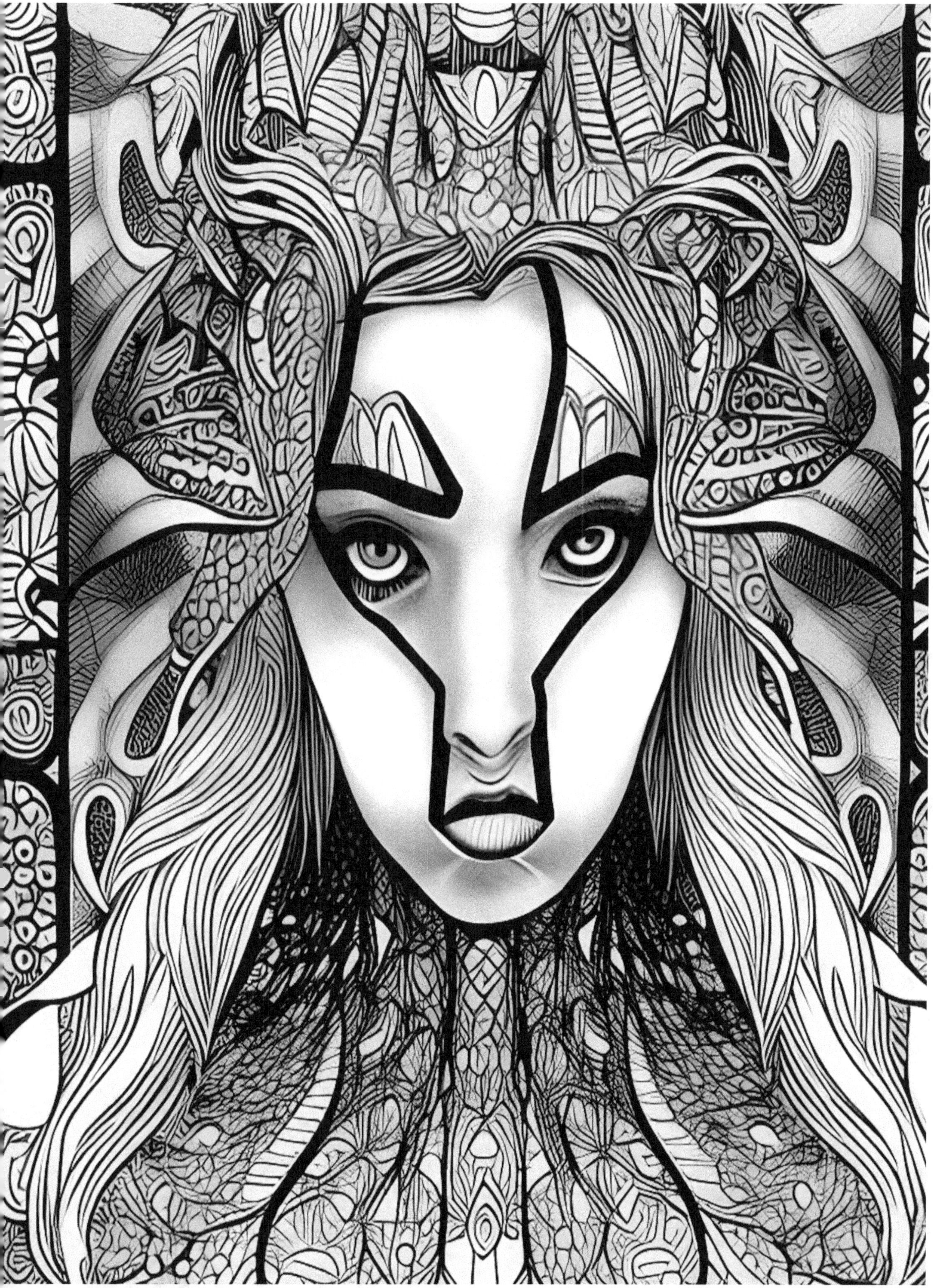

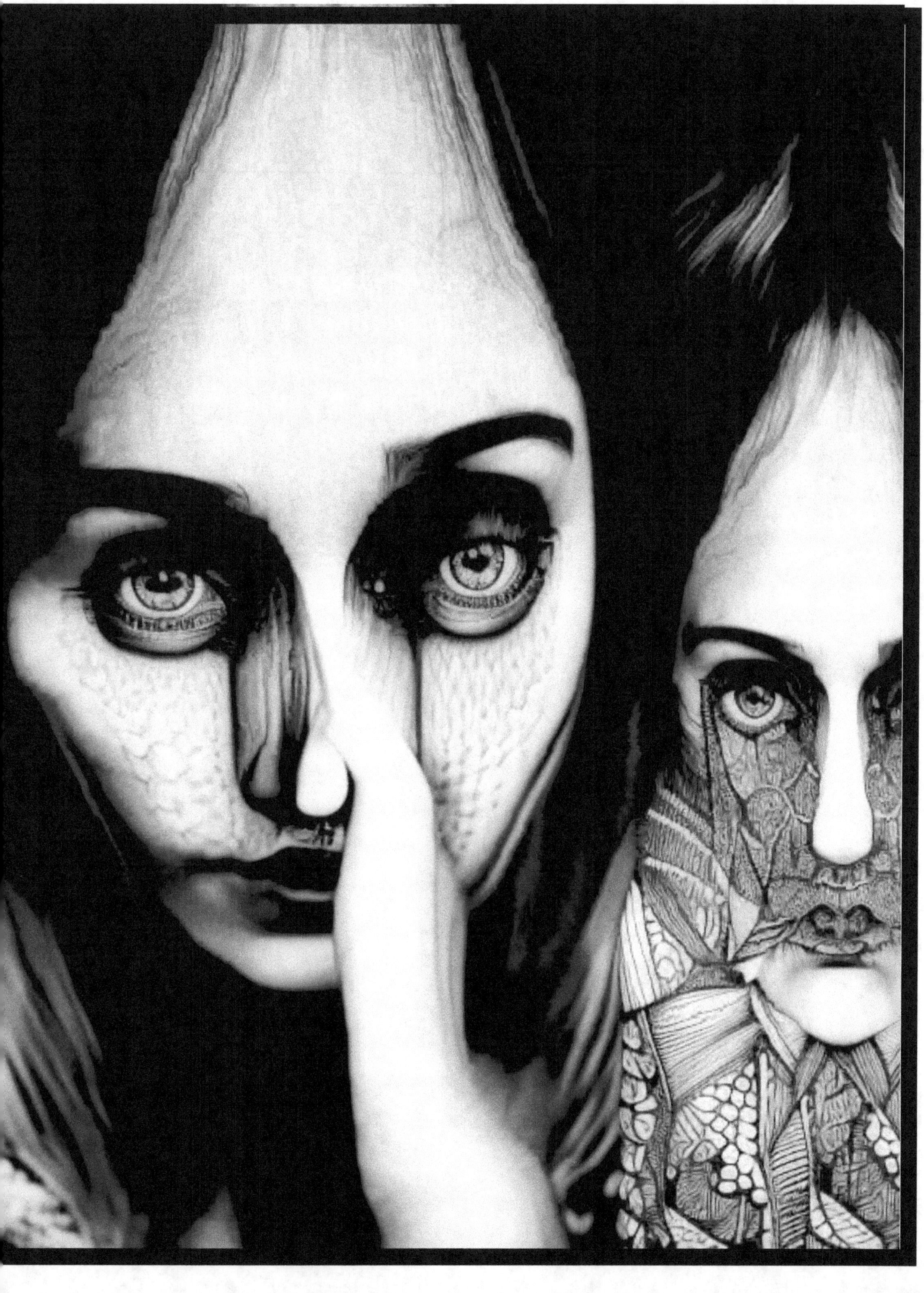

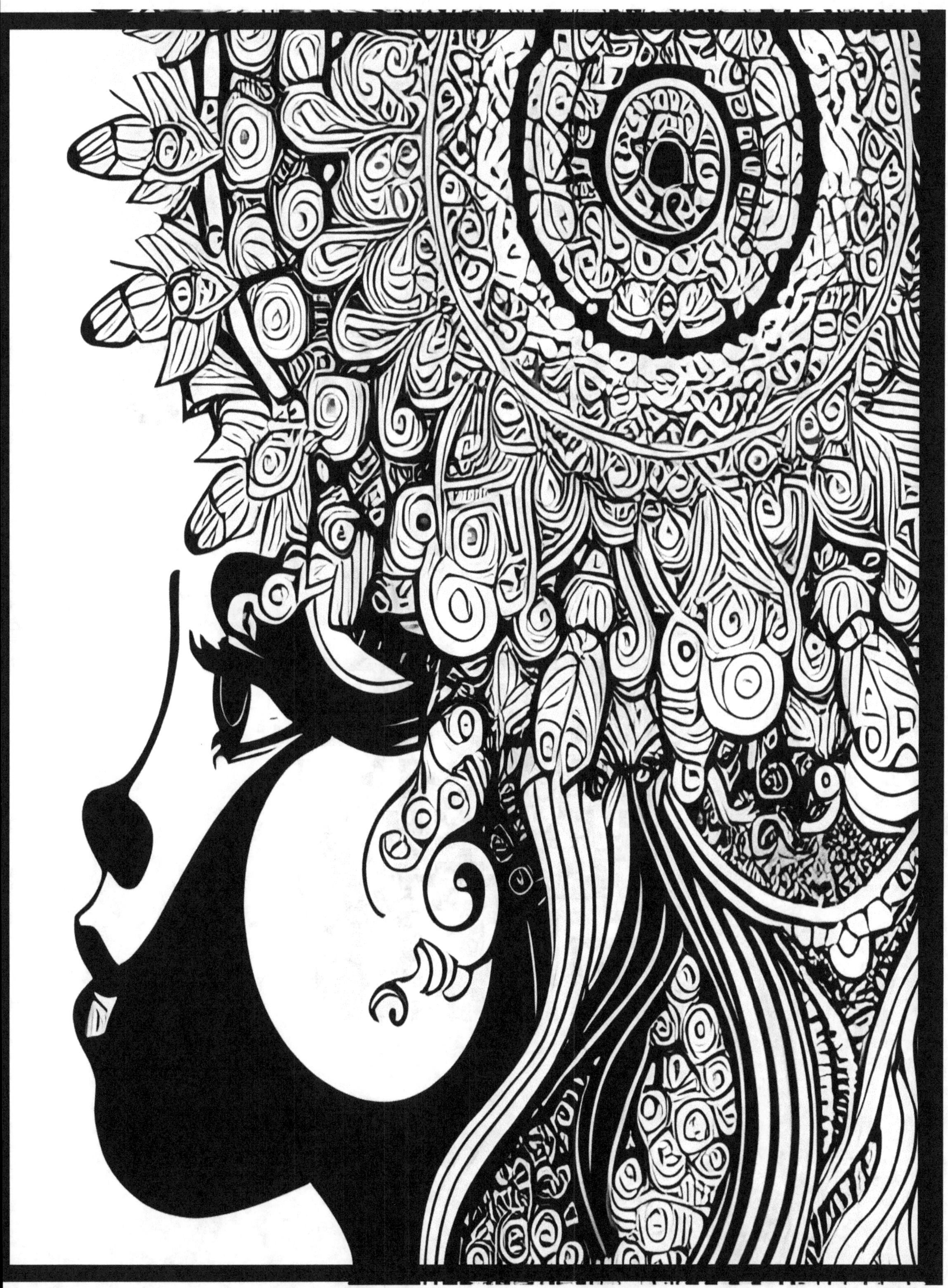

More Coming Soon

www.ingramcontent.com/pod-product-compliance
Lightning Source LLC
Chambersburg PA
CBHW080230220526
45467CB00036B/2297
* 9 7 9 8 3 8 7 7 4 7 1 8 2 *